new spanish design

new spanish design

guy julier

with 218 illustrations, 152 in colour

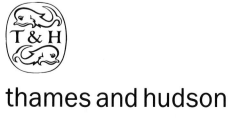

thames and hudson

For Sue and Joseph

Author's note

In Spain the surnames of both father and mother are sometimes used (*hence* Oriol Bohigas y Guardiola). In this book, however, the more common shorter version of paternal surname only is used throughout (*hence* Oriol Bohigas). Where it has been necessary to choose between Catalan and Castilian spellings of names, the author has tried as far as possible to be consistent with the most common usage in Spain itself.

© 1991 Thames and Hudson Ltd, London

Printed in Singapore

contents

introduction

7

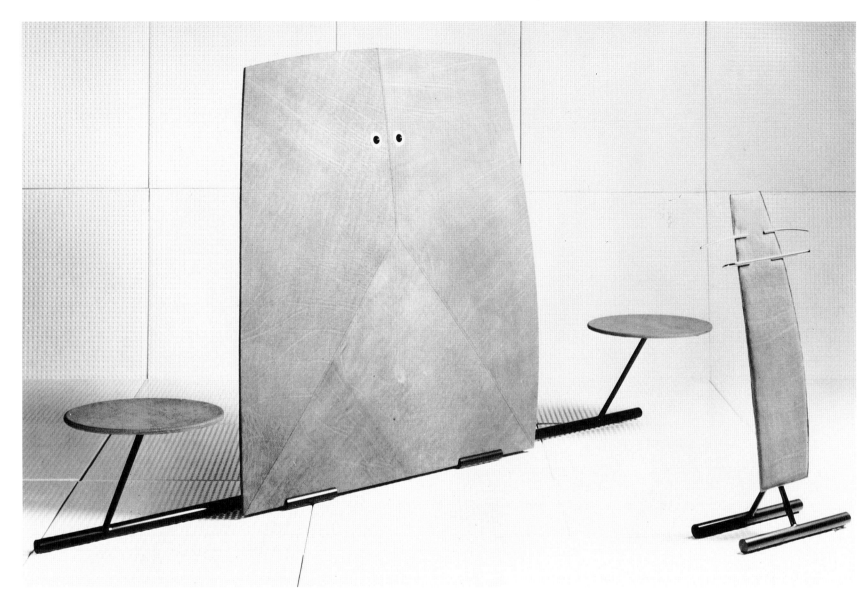

Headboard and clothes rack
Eduardo Samsó
Akaba S.A.
1986

introduction

fOLLOWING THE DEATH OF GENERAL Franco in 1975 and the subsequent transition from dictatorship to democracy, there is no doubt that Spain underwent a design boom in the 1980s. It received international acknowledgment through the growing prominence of the Spanish stands at the Milan Furniture Fair, and was also seen in the increasing numbers of buyers who found their way to the annual Valencia furniture fair. At the same time the Barcelona *bares de diseño* circuit became a unique phenomenon in contemporary design and the corporate identities of city and regional councils were radically transformed.

This design boom came on the crest of a wave of post-Francoist social, economic and cultural changes. After 1980, Spain joined NATO and the EEC, and became the seat for the Olympic Games in Barcelona, the World Fair in Seville and European Cultural Capital in Madrid, all for 1992. In 1985 the Spanish economy took a marked upturn. With these events came new patterns of consumption, new industries and a new national image.

The image of, literally, re-designing a country following thirty years of dictatorship captured the popular imagination outside Spain. The interpretation of this efflorescence, however, has led to unhelpful generalizations. Perhaps in search of the essence of a Spanish identity in design, commentators adopted approaches that were specific and a-historical, which meant that they ended up with *typical Spanish*. Spain is a nation of distinct regions. Undoubtedly the greatest concentration of designers and design activity rests in Barcelona – a fact which this book unapologetically recognizes – but in the 1990s it is becoming an increasingly regionalized affair as activity is consolidated elsewhere.

Spain's pioneering designers began working in the 1950s, before the rapid technological and industrial development of the 1960s. Another generation, who are now in their forties, were educated within radical resistance to Francoism in the late 1960s. The youngest designers have not worked under any period of dictatorship or experienced the economic depression of the 1970s, and yet are more susceptible to the myriad of influences that democratic Spain has thrown up.

This book, then, does not intend to treat Spanish design as a homogeneous entity. There is no search for the definitive Spanish style. Rather, whilst recognizing the eclecticism of Spanish design, it attempts to identify certain unifying elements within its historical development. These include the changing status and meaning of design, the influence of design education, the political solutions that design presented and the industrial structures in which it acts. Throughout, the text also recognizes the balances and tensions between the cultural and commercial interests of design.

Additionally, there can be no denying that modern Spanish design is highly subject to international influences at both ends of its history. These influences are themselves constantly subject to inflexions produced by the Spanish contexts. And it is such inflexions that give the design its significance and suggest the interest it contains. The questions at stake are: what influences are chosen, why and how are they used?

In view of the mixture of indigenous contexts and internationalist influences, the timing of the Spanish design boom is crucial. Coming after the Postmodern euphoria of Alchymia and Memphis, it was in a position to reconsider inflexions which open out new directions in design.

There is a third dimension to the influences on design in Spain, which is perhaps the hardest to gauge – the surrounding material scenery. The legacy of Gaudí, Miró and Dalí is at times plain to see. But the everyday street life of Spain is also saturated with images. Whilst its growing internationalization has brought a bombardment of foreign references to the visual vocabulary of Spain, at the same time there remain domestic details which are untouched.

New Spanish Design responds to these contexts – but it also adds to them. All the examples in this book have been produced or used. They are real. And here we find the fundamental importance of Spanish design. The concept of a design boom might suggest that we are dealing only with a fashion, but the fact remains that Spanish design is not just a series of manifestos and exhibitions: it is concerned with the actual generation and development of a fresh material culture, which has important resonances both inside and outside Spain.

Left: Coqueta chair
Stainless steel frame, leather belt, Lloyd loom seat
Pete Sans
B.D. Ediciones de Diseño
1988

Below: Mosca (fly) chair
Chrome steel, with wooden seat and backrest,
rubber upholstered
J.J. Belda
Exhibited by Luis Adelantado
1987

The design boom of the 1980s saw movements in
two directions: one was towards the recuperation of
traditional craft skills and the other was towards
forging new formal foundations.

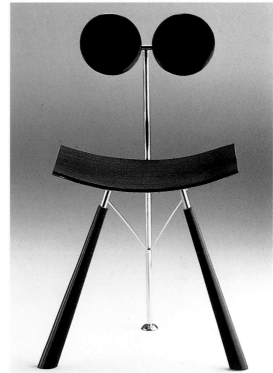

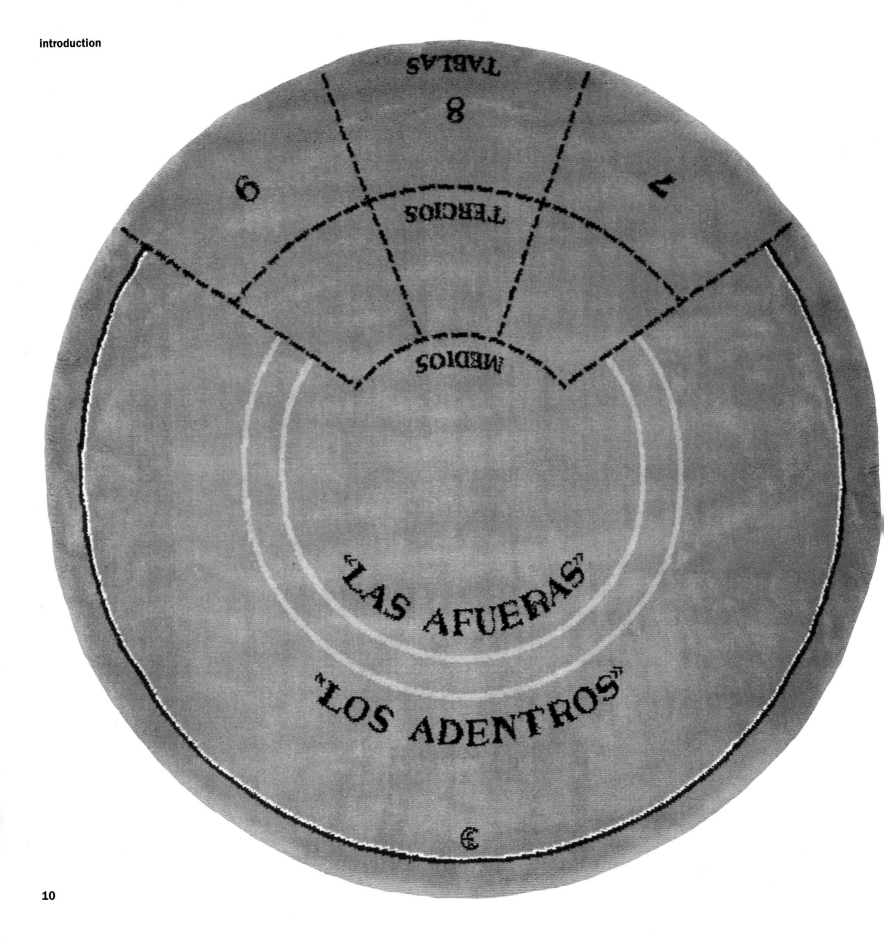

Left: A las 5 de la tarde
(At 5 p.m.) rug
Eduardo Samsó
Nani Marquina S.A.
1987

Right: Poster for
commemoration of
García Lorca
Enric Satué
1986

Among younger
designers such as
Eduardo Samsó, there is
sometimes an explicit —
if ironically playful —
statement of 'typical
Spanish'. The rug
illustrates the layout of
a bullring. Among
others, of an older
generation — such as
Enric Satué in particular
— there is a play on
visual languages
through the suggestion
and juxtaposition of
images and ideas. In
either case, strong
emphasis is laid on the
communicative element
of the design.

Above: Banco Catalano bench
Oscar Tusquets
B.D. Ediciones de Diseño
1974
Production of this bench was increased dramatically
in the 1980s when it began to be a standard feature
of renovated public spaces.

Right: Inflatable fried eggs
Marisa Gallén and Sandra Figuerola, La Nave
Torrente Industrial (TOI) S.A.
1987
Having persuaded the manufacturers of the
commercial viability of this project, Gallén and
Figuerola developed a line in 'pop' inflatables that
has proved an adventurous industrial reconversion
for them. The diameter of the eggs is 150 cms.

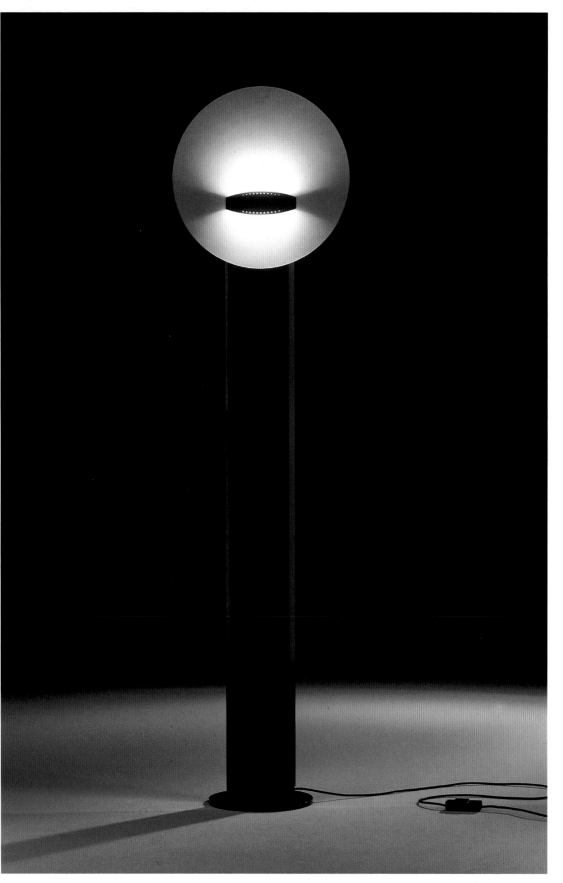

Left: Maja standard lamp
Swivelling support, with gliding dimmer
integrated into it
Sergi Devesa
Metalarte S.A.
1988
A leading producer of modern lighting in the 1960s,
Metalarte returned to an increasingly avant-garde
catalogue in the 1980s, following stagnation during
the economic crisis of the 1970s.

Above: Paco Rabanne perfume botte
André Ricard
Saint-Gobain-Desjonquères
1986

Right: Showroom of Santa & Cole S.A., furniture and
lighting editors, designed by Gabriel Ordeig,
opened 1988. Begun in 1986, Santa & Cole is in
some ways typical of many new editing companies
producing short-run high-quality furnishings
directed at the middle and upper ends of the
market.

design in history

From Art and the State to the State of the Art

Left: Calvet chair
Oak, polyurethane-varnished and
hand-carved
Antoni Gaudí
1902
Gris handed over the editing of
Gaudí furniture to B.D. Ediciones
de Diseño in 1977. Gaudí's
furniture provided an alternative
aesthetic to the Rationalist
movement.

tHE TRAJECTORY OF SPANISH HISTORY
has never been smooth, least of all during the twentieth century, in which Spain
has undergone institutional schisms and disjunctures that include two dictator-
ships, numerous failed uprisings, a civil war and two periods of renovatory
democracy. Within this wider history, design has also undergone transformations both in its internal debates and in its public status.

Since this book is about new design in Spain, emergent mostly in the 1970s
and 1980s, it might be most appropriate to look at the historical conditions
relevant to that period. However, a sense of the earlier historical construction of
design in Spain is important, above all because the shape of design, both in its
visual and more global conception, is the result of history and the experience of
it. Thus, for instance, the industrial structure in which design acted from 1970
was the result of an earlier development stretching back 150 years, if not further.
Likewise, the meaning that design had was partly the outcome of preceding
debates in the 1960s. Equally, it was about the response to the lessons learnt
from that earlier history.

To plot these transformations in the wider context of twentieth-century Spanish history is a precarious exercise, which in itself reveals the difficulties and
pitfalls of the eclectic discipline of design history. Design is as much subject to
the influences of cultural, political, social, economic and technological change as
to its internal activities and those of its designers themselves. It is therefore not
surprising to find that there invariably exist contradictions between the activity
of design and its immediate historical context in Spain, as well as the international situation. The Spanish word *desfase*, meaning, literally, 'dis-phase' or
out-of-stepness, adequately describes this condition.

Desfase existed, for instance, in the 1970s when Spain was passing through a
desperate economic crisis, but was also enjoying a cultural explosion. Similarly,
in the 1960s, Spain's design institutions were recognized internationally, but not

nationally. Earlier still, the internal policy contradictions of the Francoist government during the 1940s meant that the Modern Movement of Le Corbusier *et al* was viewed with suspicion, yet some government projects in Spain displayed distinctly Modernist tendencies. And so on. Thus, one might even venture to say that *desfase* is one of the few constants available to the historian of Spanish design as a methodological tool.

Several other constants may exist. One is that the institutional development of design has played a major role in its history. This means that the activities of design associations, schools, publications and – more recently – governmental policies towards design have been important. More than anything, their importance has been in the generation of a debate and subsequently an image of design. By extension the search for a design appropriate to Spanish cultural and economic conditions has been of fundamental importance – the choice of foreign ideas taken and modified alongside local attitudes is significant.

On the reverse side of the same coin, design has also been carried forward at a more informal, *ad hoc* level. Outside the institutional seminar rooms or the pages of design magazines, there exists another history of informal groups and movements, or individual initiatives in producing or retailing design. Such activity represents another constant. To make a complete and objective account of it is the most difficult task: given that much of it lies outside the realms of 'officialdom' and/or is of a rather submerged character, the sources for recuperating its history largely exist within the often dubious archives of oral record. In this book 'informal' initiatives are discussed within the context of chapters devoted to different design disciplines.

The relationship of the official with the unofficial account of Spanish design provides us with a final constant. We find parallels elsewhere in other analyses of design activity: formal and informal, design for day consumption and design for night consumption, Modernist and Postmodernist, and so on. The dialectic created in these relationships smacks of the *desfase* concept in the way that contradictory elements are brought together, and – in appraising Spanish design – they constantly reappear. Their character and outcome will thus unfold in the proceeding chapters. And, indeed, it is the symbiosis produced by elements within this dialectic – new, old; national, international; craft, design etc. – that creates much of the interest of Spanish design. This chapter provides the necessary preliminary by examining the wider interactions of politics, economics, culture, commerce and design in twentieth-century Spain.

As Spain began to lose its colonies at the end of the nineteenth century, two regions were becoming economically strong. One was the Basque Country, where export of iron ore to Britain in exchange for coal allowed for the develop-

Opposite: Housing block in the
calle de Muntaner, 342-348,
Barcelona
Josep Lluís Sert
1931-34
This building is Sert's first
important work and demonstrates
in particular the influence of Le
Corbusier (in whose studio Sert
had worked) on architects of the
GATCPAC group during the period
of the Second Republic. The new
architecture clearly attempted to
break from the historicist
tendencies of Modernisme and
Noucentisme.

ment of a metallurgical and shipbuilding industry. The second was Catalonia, whose industry was based on textiles and small manufacturing companies and related to the import from and export to the colonies or the Mediterranean seaboard countries.

With this gradual loss of colonies, a protectionist plan was instituted from 1892 and was reinforced in 1907 when a law forbade the import of goods that were already being produced by companies connected with the state. Thus the seeds of state intervention in industry were sown way before the Francoist dictatorship. However, in April 1931 the conservative interests that had ruled Spain since 1875, first by manipulating the electoral machinery of the constitutional monarchy, then under the relatively benign dictatorship of General Primo de Rivera from 1923 to 1930, suddenly found themselves bereft of any institutional protection, having lost monarchist seats in all the great cities of Spain. King Alfonso XIII left Spain – declaring, 'It seems that we are out of fashion' – and a democratic republic of Spain was established.

Any summary of the period 1931-39, about which an estimated 16,000 books have been written, will over-simplify, but it is clear that the general character was of equivocation and revolution, followed by civil war. The socialists and communists failed to gain the political foothold that might have been predicted, whilst the Marxist POUM and the Anarchist CNT attempted, and succeeded in places, in creating a permanent state of revolution, seizing land and factories. Within this restless revolutionary activity, we find the energetic development of the GATEPAC and GATCPAC groups. As groups of architects dedicated to the promotion of the Modern Movement in Spain, their aims struck a chord with socialist politicians, particularly in Barcelona, which subsequently allowed the development of some spectacular Modernist housing schemes, such as GATC-PAC's Casa Bloc in Sant Andreu (1934).

At the same time, whilst the Basque Country had consolidated her heavy papermaking and metallurgical industries from 1900, in Catalonia we find a shift from her classic first industrial revolution base of textiles, construction and metal transformation towards lighter and more varied industries producing consumer goods. Without a raw-materials base, Catalonia's industrial development was characteristic of similar countries such as Sweden or Switzerland. Furthermore, such was the economic and demographic concentration of Catalonia and the Basque Country that, by 1930, the *per capita* consumption was equal to four times that of the rest of Spain. Thus with the disparity of demand between these regions and the rest of the internal market, Catalonia in particular was to orientate its sales of consumer goods more to the rest of Europe.

This industrial development was carried through the period of the Second Republic. In the meantime, a broad coalition of monarchists, the Catholic

church, Italian-style fascists – the Falangists – and the Army gathered strength. In July 1936, General Francisco Franco left his post in the Canary Islands to take up position as leader of this coalition and Spain was thrown into three devastating years of Civil War.

The Civil War ended on 1 April 1939 and General Franco was installed as dictator of a nation whose agricultural production had dropped by a third, half of whose railway rolling stock had been lost, but whose industrial sector remained mostly intact – the Anarchists burned churches, not factories.

The kind of government that followed is best described as a government of autarchy and interventionism rather than of straightforward fascism. Whilst the Falangists were not greatest in numbers on the Nationalist side, their standard was dominant economically until 1959 and culturally beyond that date. One of the most significant new laws, in terms of the organization of society, was one of the first passed by the Nationalist government. It followed closely what had been inscribed in the constitution of the Falangists in 1934, which itself read as follows:

> We conceive the economic organization of Spain in terms of a gigantic union of producers. We shall organize Spanish society on a corporative basis by means of a system of vertical syndicates, arranged in accordance with the various branches of production in the service of the national economic integrity.

Thus, the conflicts endemic in capitalist, liberal democracy would be harmonized by the setting up of vertical trade unions of national syndicalism. This 'harmonization' included on the one hand the denial of the right to strike, but on the other attempted to lump the classes together into a great 'nation of producers'. With it came the establishment in 1939 of the Instituto Nacional de Industria (INI), which was to extend the influence of the state in the economy by acting as a national investment organization, supporting industries it felt necessary – these being, notably, the heavy raw-material-based industries (of which there were an abundance), at the expense of lighter industries that would have required the import of capital goods.

Imports were made virtually impossible by extremely high tariffs, the onus being on the revitalization of existing industries and the tentative creation of new industries for a home market. These objectives were also achieved through stringent state control of the economy under two laws of late 1939, the *Protección y fomento de la industria nacional* and the *Ordenación y defensa de la industria nacional*, under which industry connected with defence was strengthened and state authorization was required for either the setting up of, or the expansion of, or investment in, new factories.

The dominant idea of this autarchy and interventionism, then, was to create an isolated Nationalist state in which the good peasant tills the land and the factory worker tightens the bolt of the state machinery. Spain would be, to quote the *Proteción y fomento de la industria nacional*, redeemed, from the importation of exotic products'.

This situation had important resonances in architecture and design. Firstly, the virtual stagnation of the Spanish economy meant that there barely existed a market for new products, nor any industrial apparatus appropriate for developing them. Whilst other European countries embarked on postwar reconstruction in the late 1940s and 1950s, Spain was to remain in post-Civil War poverty. Secondly, and equally importantly, Francoist cultural policy during the Autarchy was not sympathetic to avant-garde propositions in art, architecture and design.

An accurate exposition of this cultural ideology is to be found in a treatise by E. Giménez Caballero on art and architecture, published in 1935 and entitled *Arte y Estado*. Giménez Caballero was a rampantly pro-Francoist poet, whose publications encapsulated the vigorous and vacuous official rhetoric of the early years of Francoist rule. In *Arte y Estado* Giménez Caballero's view of the use of the avant-garde is equivocal. On the one hand, he proposed that art consisted primarily of painting and sculpture, which barely interested anyone any more. If you wanted to immortalize your loves, or your travels, you used a Kodak rather than bought a painting; architecture, useful art, cinema, the radio, the graphic arts and propaganda were more appropriate to modern times. The avant-garde had failed; it was in a state of despair; and it was represented by those around Picasso whose despair was the 'last romantic and liberal position in the West, the refuge of the self lost in space'. On the other hand, whilst being a confirmed mass 'culture-vulture' (he described an advertisement with a plate of ham and eggs as 'magical, fascinating and provocative'), he still had a certain hope for the likes of Picasso and Le Corbusier.

Certainly, he argued, the so-called New Architecture of Gropius and Mies van de Rohe was created by 'the Jewish, socialist spirit and the teachings of 1917', but he believed that salvation rested in the sisterhood of Italy and Spain, with their Catholic genius, where a tradition of functionality would lead to a 'stark, massive and proportional architecture'. He was referring to a functionality that was to be found as much in Imperial as in Rationalist architecture. By and large, it was a hybrid Imperial style of architecture that would extol the glory of Francoist Spain. This was trumpeted by an extraordinary government treatise to architecture students, the *Manifiesto de la Alhambra*, published in 1953, which champions the Alhambra of Granada as a model for the creation of a true national architecture. Nevertheless, in the same way that the Francoist govern-

Right: 'Gratacels Urquinaona',
Barcelona
Luis Gutiérrez Soto
1936-42

Centre and far right: Banco
Vitalicio de España, Barcelona
Luis Bonet
1942-50

'Gratacels Urquinaona'
demonstrates a knowledge of
central-European functionalist
grammar; its architect, Gutiérrez
Soto, from Madrid, went on in the
1940s to design the Ministerio del
Aire de Madrid, the building most
representative of Francoist
monumentalism. 'Gratacels
Urquinaona', therefore, reflected
the possibility of appropriating
functionalist typologies within the
regime. The Banco Vitalicio de
España demonstrates the
monumental classicism found in
many buildings of the Autarchy.

ment itself was made up of a hybrid of differing interests, it is also difficult to find consistency with regards cultural policy. Thus, there would also be room for Rationalist architecture within the Francoist scheme, just as Rationalism was appropriated in Mussolini's Italy.

Essentially, the Rationalism that was identified with Le Corbusier (and thus with the GATCPAC group of the Second Republic) had its place. Whilst apparently some rationalist buildings were 'covered up' just after the Civil War to hide the unfortunate and 'horrific cubist' architecture, the latter's massive starkness might be reconciled with the gestural monumentality of the Francoist, or rather Falangist, rhetoric.

The avant-garde was obsolete in the face of mass culture; it also constituted a 'red threat'. Yet it could perhaps be useful if it produced the appropriate works. If there was to be an avant-garde at all, then it should be controlled and appropriated. Government rural housing schemes, forming part of a highly limited post-Civil War redevelopment scheme, showed peculiarly 'Modern Movement' tendencies in conception. However, much of Spain's cultural avant-garde, including the painter Joan Miró and the architects Josep Lluís Sert and Antoni Bonet, had already gone into exile at the end of the Civil War. With the cultural continuity broken, it would take another generation to pick up the pieces.

It was during these barren years of the 1940s and 50s that we find the first tentative steps towards a modern design consciousness in Spain. Returning from exile in Montpellier in 1946, the art critic and historian, graphic designer and design theorist, Alexandre Cirici, published a seminal article entitled 'L'art de la saviesa' (the art of the familiar) in the clandestine Catalan magazine, *Ariel*. The magazine itself was created by a group of Barcelonese intellectuals dedicated to the reclamation and promotion of the Catalan avant-garde. In this article Cirici argued that 'One should give no lesser a place in culture to record players, the toilet, the fork, the hat, the bottle, than the monument.' The article itself is essentially a compact essay on Modernism, demonstrating how Cézanne and Picasso had begun to look at objects as they really are, but where possible showing that various Catalan artists and writers had similarly been affected by the developments of the machine age. Thus it may be read as a deliberate political gesture, aligning the avant-garde, historically and contemporaneously, with the European avant-garde, as well as using Modernism as a rejection of Francoism: the article implies that whilst taking up a Modernist position meant the objective analysis of phenomena, Francoism evaded, mystified and iconographied. Thus, as an antidote to the heroic gesture of the 'Cara al Sol' (face to the sun, the Falangist anthem), the Modernist should interest himself with the everyday, 'from the toilet' to 'the bottle'. In 1955 Cirici also wrote a thesis on the history of industrial design at the University of Barcelona, though it was barely considered a serious subject by the university authorities.

Another individual who was preoccupied with the toilet and the bottle in these early days was André Ricard. Whilst in London in the early 1950s to learn English, Ricard was exposed to the growing design movement stemming from the 1951 Festival of Britain. He returned to Spain with 'ideas that at that time seemed completely futuristic' and was able to continue his interest in design with his family firm, where sometimes he was able to design 'humble' objects. Feeling somewhat of a 'Robinson Crusoe' on a design-dry island, he put himself in contact with Raymond Loewy in 1956, having read his *Ugly Things Don't Sell*.

In contrast to Cirici, André Ricard came to industrial design mostly through practice. He spent very little time in Spain during the 1950s, and it was really through his experience outside Spain that he was able to define and make sense of what he was doing. Within Spain, there were others who began practising industrial design without necessarily defining it as such. One such example is the company Soler i Palau, who started manufacturing electric fans in 1951. Another example is Miguel Milà, who despite having studied architecture came to industrial design via interior design and started to explore 'the scarce possibilities which industry had to offer to the designer … through personal interest', and really, 'without knowing exactly what design was'.

Butterfly chair
Antoni Bonet, Juan Kurchan and
Jorge Ferrari-Hardoy
1939
The Barcelonese architect, Antoni Bonet, joined the subsequent co-designers of the famous Butterfly chair in the studio of Le Corbusier in Paris in 1937. From there they moved to Argentina, where the chair was conceived. Whilst it definitely has antecedents stretching back to nineteenth-century Britain and was manufactured internationally (an estimated 5 million were sold in the USA during the 1950s alone), it none the less took on the symbolic value of the 'design that could have been' in Spain if the Rationalist triumphs had continued after the Second Republic.

Given the underdeveloped state of Spanish industry and the suppression of cultural avant-garde initiatives during this period, it is hardly surprising that the consolidation of the concept of design should be carried strongly at a theoretical level rather than at a practical level.

Much of the theoretical debate on design was formulated in architectural circles. The teaching of architecture in Spain's only architectural schools in the 1950s, in Barcelona and Madrid, was eminently conservative, with little interest in the New Architecture being taught and practised in the rest of Europe and the United States. Grouped around the Colegio de Arquitectos de Cataluña y Baleares in Barcelona, however, were some architects who formed Grup R, which was destined to continue the Rationalist project of the GATCPAC era. Grup R was a coalition of architects, brought together to promote their collective aims through exhibitions, seminars and publications. Its members included Antoni de Moragas, Josep Antoni Coderch, Frederico Correa, Alfons Milà (brother of Miguel Milà) and Oriol Bohigas. Apart from the isolated occasion of Coderch's housing scheme, the Spain of the Autarchy was not to allow the breadth of projects carried out by the GATCPAC group during the 1930s. The projects of the members of Grup R were often limited to single homes, particularly in the coastal towns north and south of Barcelona, such as Sitges and Cadaques. Under the influence of Coderch, in particular, the Rationalist project was subject to inflexions, bringing local vernacular styles to the architecture. In addition, since fittings and furniture were not available in Spain to match the technical and aesthetic standards demanded, these architects took to designing themselves. In the same way that Cirici called for attention to be paid to the material world, and Ricard starting designing 'humble' objects, so a few architects were led to producing design on a small, individualistic scale. Thus, almost by force of circumstances, these architects played an important role in the early stages of design in Spain and shaping its character.

Returning from his visit to Raymond Loewy in 1956, André Ricard contacted Antoni de Moragas, having heard that he too was involved in industrial design. Antoni de Moragas had known the Italian architect, Gio Ponti, via various international architecture conferences and it was at a dinner with him and André Ricard that Ponti suggested that some kind of industrial design organization should be set up in Spain to bring together the diaspora of industrial designers. Thus the Instituto de Diseño Industrial de Barcelona (IDIB) was formed in 1957; and in 1959 Ricard travelled to Stockholm for the first congress of the International Council of Societies of Industrial Design (ICSID).

However, whilst IDIB was recognized outside Spain, it was not quite so lucky within the country. In this period of Francoism, all societal activity underwent controls and censorship; all meetings of more than ten people required permis-

Housing for metallurgical workers, Barcelona
Oriol Bohigas and Josep Mª Martorell
1958-59
This building, by leading Grup R members Bohigas and Martorell, on the one hand exists within the ideology of 'Rational housing' (in line with the precepts of the International Movement) and yet, on the other, was constructed entirely using local techniques and materials. This mixture came to be called 'Realist Architecture' and reflects both Italian and local preoccupations of its time.

Copehagen ashtrays
Plastic
André Ricard
Flamagas S.A.
Designed 1966
Still in production in the 1990s, these ashtrays are typical of the 'humble' design that Ricard learnt and championed throughout his long career.

sion. IDIB was dealt its death blow by the refusal of central government to recognize it as a society, thereby making it illegal. The argument in the government's reply to IDIB's application for official recognition was that it could not accept its statutes 'whilst within them, one of their objectives was to found an association for professional designers [which was] the proper role of the [National] Syndical Organization'.

The solution to this problem was for industrial designers to append themselves to a pre-existing organization. Thus in March 1960 the Agrupación de Diseño Industrial (ADI) was formed as part of the Fometo de las Artes Decorativas (FAD) to make ADIFAD. FAD had existed in Barcelona as a decorative arts institution since 1903. It offered an infrastructure to which other interest groups later added themselves, including graphic designers, who created ADGFAD in 1961.

In 1961, ADIFAD was accepted as a member organization of ICSID. This automatically gave ADIFAD an interesting status. It was recognized outside Spain, and took advantage of all the benefits that resulted, whilst inside Spain it received no official aid or recognition. It was marginalized but also independent within Spain. It was not national, but it was international. This ambiguous position continued through the economic and social changes of the 1960s; indeed, it can be said as much of the institutional status of design as of the status of the objects themselves.

The effects of such a protectionist economic policy were largely catastrophic. By 1956 the Spanish economy could not expand any further (expansion had in any case been relative – it was not until 1948 that industrial production surpassed its 1929 level). Inflation was at 16 per cent and Spain's foreign exchange reserve was exhausted.

The knights in shining chrome armour who saved the economy from oblivion were a new team of technocrats of the Opus Dei, who were appointed to the Ministry by Franco in 1959. This hierarchical international Catholic sect set up the University of Navarra in 1962, as well as a very high-powered business school in Barcelona called IESE. Its money could be found in everything from publishing houses to textiles companies. Suddenly, the economic health of the nation was pushed to the forefront of the public imagination. Economists such as Ramón Tamanes, Fuentes Quitana, Rojo Duque and Antonio Robert became household names and in 1963 *España Económica* reported:

> Economic problems never before attracted the attention they are receiving today in our country... In the opinion of many sociologists, the activity that these problems have provoked, previously restricted to a clique of professionals ... shows the political good health of the Spanish people.

Crowds in Barcelona's Ramblas await the appearance of the newspapers, 22 November 1966, following Franco's pronouncement of the *Ley Orgánico*, which purported to allow limited syndical representation in the government.

Of the finer details of economy, however, little was known and certainly access to its planning was restricted to those who sat at the top of public and syndical bureaucracies, those with recognized places in the hierarchy of corporations and banking, a handful of intellectuals and private entrepreneurs with long-established links with public authorities.

The bottom line of what the new ministry of Opus Dei technocrats proposed was economic growth at whatever cost. Import restrictions were lowered to encourage the inflow of foreign capital, capital goods and tourists. Spain made an unsuccessful attempt to join the Common Market in 1962 (though Britain's application was rejected in the same year). Within Spain, the restrictive economic laws instigated by the Falangists were loosened, if not done away with.

The performance of the economy during the years that followed was dramatic. Between 1961 and 1973, a period often referred to as the *años de desarollo* (years of development), the economy grew at an average rate of 7 per cent – faster than any non-socialist country except Japan. Incomes also quadrupled over this period. When judged in comparison with other Western countries, such a growth rate may not be exceptionally impressive; similar figures may be registered in nearly all Western countries at the same time. However, given the fact that Spain was coming from far behind the others, then the 1960s may be justly called the years of the 'economic miracle'.

Thus, the domestic landscape of Spain changed radically. Between 1961 and 1975, according to the Fundación Foessa, the number of telephones per 1000 people leapt from 60 to 195, cars from 12 to 111, TVs from 9 to 260 – and so on. From 1960 to 1970, the percentage of town dwellers in towns of more than 50,000 rose from 35 to 44. In 1967, 22.3 per cent of homes in Barcelona had been constructed in the previous six years.

Yet the statistics need putting in a wider context. With the changes came the concept of the Two Spains (rather like the Two Italies). The 'economic miracle' (or 'development at all costs' – depending on the way you look at it) entailed huge movements of population from the poorer rural regions, such as Andalucia and Galicia, to the large cities, in particular, Barcelona, Bilbao and Madrid. In the case of Barcelona, the increase in population as the result of migration between 1951 and 1960 was 450,000, some 18 per cent; this figure doubled between 1960 and 1970. There was also a vast outflux of workers to other European countries; between 1960 and 1973 over one million were given official assistance in seeking work abroad. The overall result was, on the one hand, a Spain of a depopulated and depressed countryside, on the other, a Spain of wealthier, but in some respects squalid, industrial cities.

If average incomes did quadruple from 1961 to 1973, their distribution remained fairly much the same – the rich got richer, and the poor went up a notch.

Nuns administer Coca-Cola and hamburgers to 600 children in Gràcia, Barcelona, 18 August 1960.

Similarly, a comparison of consumption figures provided by the Foessa Foundation shows that Spain reached per capita consumption levels in terms of televisions, cars, telephones, kilowatts, steel etc. in 1973 that had already been attained by Italy between 5 and 10 years before, by France some 10 years before or more, and by the USA between 30 and 50 years before.

Mass consumption of, let us say, low-culture goods and ideas underpinned state control in this period. Whilst in the 1940s and 50s the ideal state was one where 'the good peasant tills the land and the factory worker tightens the bolt of the state machinery', the state of the 1960s was spoon-fed on 'cars, television and football'. Having lost its great writers, film-makers, architects and artists who were either dead (as in the case of García Lorca) or in exile (as in the case of Josep Lluís Sert), the state continued to encourage an effective 'culture of evasion' – evasion, that is, from the alienation of living in an immigrant suburb, from the long working week and from the temptation towards class struggle. The regime did not directly create pulp culture for the masses; rather, it left unfettered the private interests that monopolized the market.

The culture of evasion was a culture of reception as much as evasion, meaning that it was very much dominated by the import of cultural goods rather than by home production, and that, even within home production, participation was limited and mass passive consumption was encouraged. Thus anything provocative, political or avant-garde was viewed with mistrust. In contrast to this, designing – for the few who were involved in the activity – symbolized a creative act which would counter such passivity.

The consumption and production of material goods registered a high degree of homespun lamelessness and Euro-dependency, too. Whilst imports of consumer goods remained fairly small – the high import tariffs on such goods strongly discouraging them – the goods manufactured inside Spain and filling the vacuum were almost exclusively made under licence from foreign companies, or were poor re-hashes of foreign products. Research and development was almost non-existent. An OECD report on Spain in 1971 revealed that, nationally, the sum spent on research was 0.27 per cent of the GNP as compared with 2-4 per cent in other member countries.

At the same time the networks between company directors, bankers and government ministers laced together by Opus Dei continued in the longer term the pre-1959 tradition of supporting economic lame ducks, such as the steel industry at one end, while releasing only enough capital for a multitude of tiny firms at the other – in 1973, 80 per cent of companies had less than 5 employees. In short, the state dominance of the economy led to the survival of the clumsy giants and the stunted growth of its smaller industries.

Within this context, design was naturally anathema to the dominant prevailing cultural and economic currents. Firstly, design represented aesthetic and technological investigation. In 1961, ADIFAD set up its Delta design awards on the lines of the Italian Compasso d'Oro prizes. Reviewing these awards in 1968, Oriol Bohigas complained of 'the lack of creativity of our industry, and the economic and ideological meanness of our commerce that still hasn't managed to seize the reins of a consumer society and are content to work with scandalously shabby products or dishonest copies of any old foreign thing'.

Bohigas also warned against the danger of prostituting design to the purposes of marketing, thereby losing all aesthetic and ethical value. Secondly, therefore, design, for its leading exponents, signified a certain moral position in face of the chaos of the consumer society of the *años de desarollo*. For the members of FAD, design was anything but 'typical Spanish'. It avoided the 'typical Spanish' of the myth of folkloric Spain that the Francoist government promoted in parallel to the technological development of the 1960s. It was not about bullfighting, castanets, or even the 'Spanish fury' said to characterize its football teams.

Nor was design concerned with the 'typical Spanish' of shoddy consumer items produced under foreign licences. Notions of nationalism, when applied to consumer items, were complex. Spain's consumer boom in the 1960s was its *first* nationwide consumer boom. In such conditions, consumer choice and demand were limited: new products constantly monopolized the market (indeed, there was a waiting list for SEAT cars during the 1960s). This situation was accentuated by import protection, as well as by Spain's cultural isolation. Thus, by and large, the Spanish market *made do* with the little choice that was on offer,

The people's car: a SEAT 600 is blessed on St Christopher's Day, 1968.

rather than rejected it out of hand. Many of the products on offer were of foreign design, though since they were of Spanish manufacture, they had no particular international signification. On a more general level, however, there did exist a distinct perception of the foreign. This could have been a view of foreign depravity imported by tourists to the Mediterranean coast, or carried by foreign films that undermined the official view of life, but it could also represent a glamorous 'other'.

The consequences were problematic for design. In 1965 Lluís Domènech, while reviewing the ADIFAD awards, criticized some of the winning products, including some ice-pincers by Miguel Milà, for their 'James Bond design'. This view was echoed by architects, in particular Oriol Bohigas. By the mid-1960s some Barcelonese architects viewed the recent architecture of Mies and Johnson as an appropriation of the Bauhaus spirit which resulted merely in empty abstraction; they were building *chic* modern offices for the interests of capital rather than responding to the demands of social concern. And in Spain of the development years, with its massive internal immigration and chaotic infrastructure, planned housing schemes were more appropriate to the demands of social concern than 'James Bond design'. In the meantime, by avoiding either the constraints of industry or the myths of folkloric Spanish nationhood, design was to be international. In becoming so, it not only ran the risk of reproducing this myth of the glamorous 'other', but also of being elitist and inappropriate to the demands of Spanish society. In addition, design was about objects for a consumer society, whilst many of the designers themselves were opposed to the consumer society as it existed.

These problems did not necessarily plunge design into constant crisis during the 1960s. For the few designers that were active in this period, the major question was finding enough work. Nor were the problems exclusive to Spain. Moral issues in design came under increasing scrutiny by many designers throughout Europe and America during this period. Nevertheless, given the Spanish context – dictatorship, accompanied by a certain kind of economic boom – these problems perhaps became more urgent, and took on an immediately more weighty political nature. Certainly the development of a design method appropriate to these local conditions was to pass through several significant stages, with lasting effects.

Alongside the design institutes, such as ADIFAD, the Barcelona of the 1960s saw the establishment of Spain's first design schools. In 1959, under Alexandre Cirici's direction, there began an experimental school under the auspices of FAD to teach graphic, interior and industrial design. (In the same year, graphic design was incorporated into the subjects offered by the crafts-dominated Massana school in Barcelona.) Stemming from discussion by artists and designers about the problems of live art under the pressures of official art, the method of the FAD school was to be based on what was known of the Bauhaus and the present activities of Ulm, that is roughly, the understanding of form and function, and also of materials and precedents.

When the FAD school fell into financial difficulties in 1961, Elisava was formed as a replacement, with the financial backing of the Centro de Influencia Católica Feminina (CICF). Right from the beginning the school lent great importance to conceptual and theoretical aspects, with Alexandre Cirici, Xavier Rubert de Ventos, the philosopher of aesthetics, and the cultural historian, Romà Gubern, acting at its core. Like the FAD school, Elisava followed a methodological line informed by the Bauhaus and subsequently by its Ulm revision from 1950 to 1968 under Max Bill and his successor as Director, Tomás Maldonado, who was a frequent visitor to Barcelona.

In 1966, however, a schism within Elisava precipitated the walk-out of virtually its entire staff to form a new design school, Eina. The academic year of 1964-65 in Barcelona had seen a profound growth in student unrest centred around the University but permeating into other teaching establishments. Within Elisava, there was a growing concern amongst teachers about the increasingly conservative position of its supporting institution, the CICF, and the latter's intervention in college affairs. This was brought to a head when the CICF excluded from the teaching staff some known radical teachers, including Oriol Bohigas. Their final response in September 1966 was mass resignation.

By November 1966, the resignees had formulated a curriculum for the new school to be called Eina. Eina was to be entirely financed from its own fees and the pockets of its founders. Thus it would have complete autonomy from any official institutional body. It was also to break from the Ulm-dominated methods of Elisava and formulate its own philosophy. This was to be much more appropriate to the local needs of design and, at the same time, to have lasting resonances for the shape of Spanish design. Among its first students were Josep Lluscà, Ramón Isern, Gemma Bernal, Pepe Cortés, Carlos Riart and Beth Galí; and its staff included the graphic designer América Sánchez, the painter Albert Ràfols Casamada, the architect Frederico Correa, Romà Gubern and, of course, Alexandre Cirici. Many of these staff had been marginalized, or even expelled – as in Frederico Correa's case – from university activity. Many of the students, such as Josep Lluscà and Pepe Cortés, had come from brief and unsatisfying encounters with architecture.

At the start the school really only had one member of staff – Joan Antoni Blanc – who had had a specific training in industrial design. Otherwise, its curriculum was distinctly humanistic and diverse. The intellectual pace of Eina was set in February 1967 by the visit of the group of Italian intellectuals known as Gruppo 63. Their visit was organized by Cirici and consisted of three intensive days of seminars. Gruppo 63 included Umberto Eco and Gillo Dorfles and was complemented by a group of Spanish and Catalan speakers which included Alexandre Cirici, the architects Oscar Tusquets, Frederico Correa, Oriol Bohigas and Ricardo Bofill, and the painters Albert Ràfols Casamada and Antoni Tàpies, as well as several poets. Much of the discussion during these three days centred on linguistics and structuralism. Semiotics and the theory of information were not necessarily brand new to those of Eina: at Elisava, Ràfols Casamada had run a course on the Theory of Information in the academic year of 1964-65 and Cirici had been teaching semiotics since he had first read *Opera Aperto* by Umberto Eco in 1963. However, the presence of such a large and prestigious group of Italian intellectuals in Barcelona became a catalyst for the wider adoption of the linguistic approach to phenomena.

Discussion spills out of the seminar room and into the sun at the 1971 ICSID conference in Ibiza.

Structuralist and semiotic readings, and an interest in mass culture, were becoming increasingly popular throughout Spain's universities towards the end of the 1960s. They provided a critique of society which went beyond a traditional Marxist viewpoint, the latter being seen as no longer relevant to a communication-saturated society; and at the same time, they provided a critique which lay beyond the comprehension of the government censor. In design terms, they also provided a radical alternative to the ideology of Modernism.

While the Modernist project of the International Movement was taken on board through the writings of Alexandre Cirici, the architecture of Grup R and

Studio Per, September 1968. Left to right: Pep Bonet, Oscar Tusquets, Cristian Cirici, Lluís Clotet.

at Elisava, it would always be subject to modifications. The debate about where to take it next was particularly strong amongst architects descended from Grup R, who became known in the late 1960s as the Escuela de Barcelona, a loose coalition that included the studio Martorell-Bohigas-Mackay, Correa-Milà and Lluís Domènech, and Studio Per comprising Oscar Tusquets, Lluís Clotet, Pep Bonet and Cristian Cirici. Since architecture had the advantage of being a university-based subject, its theoretical standpoints were invariably developed first amongst these architects and then communicated through to designers. In a repeat of the experience of Grup R, these architects had been largely excluded from large projects in favour of Madrid-based architects, which in turn led them to work on a smaller scale. In addition they had a natural propensity for working on detail, which was largely inherited from the Modernista tradition. In Catalonia, with its own distinct Art Nouveau movement at the end of the nineteenth and the beginning of the twentieth centuries, designers worked naturally on all forms of expression, applied on scales as diverse as Gaudí's massive Sagrada Família and furniture. Thus the Escuela de Barcelona was able to carry its experience in both theoretical and practical terms into design.

Of course the relevance of the Modernist project of the International Movement to postwar conditions, particularly in Mediterranean countries, had been raised by architects in Italy, such as Gio Ponti, in the early 1950s. A need for a

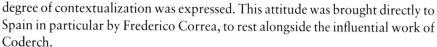

Ibiza ICSID, 1971. Instant City to house participants (left); involvement in Antoni Miralda's opening ceremony (right).

degree of contextualization was expressed. This attitude was brought directly to Spain in particular by Frederico Correa, to rest alongside the influential work of Coderch.

By the time of the Gruppo 63 seminar, the visual languages that concerned the designer were diverse, going beyond the Coderchian incorporation of local vernacular styles into Rationalism. Modernista, Classical, Pop or ironic references to 'typical Spanish' could be made. Semiotics and structuralism not only presented a way of decoding the images of society, they provided a tool for the very subversion of those images. Thus, the designer could draw from an eclectic array of images, re-contextualise them, reconstruct them, or subvert them.

Such an approach smacks of conceptual art. Indeed, alongside design activities, Eina in its earlier years was an important focal point for conceptual artists, including Jordi Benito, Ferran García-Sevilla and Antoni Llena. It was also as much a centre for film criticism, literature and cultural analysis. During its first five years, the activities of Eina included publications, happenings, theme parties, seminars, debates and even the – in its time – statutory student strike. Situated in a converted house on the hills above Barcelona, it provided a meeting point for the marginalized and self-marginalized artistic and design avant-garde. Its broad, conceptually based teaching thus turned out designers who perhaps lacked a strong technical training, and yet had an intellectual versatility and were unabashed in turning their hands to a variety of design disciplines. Thus, at Eina an appropriate methodology for design in Spain was arrived at.

Whilst the intake of Eina was limited to around 45 students a year, it provided the impulse for a flurry of design activities. In this respect 1971 represents an important year. ADIFAD had been elected to organize the 1971 ICSID conference. They chose Ibiza as the location for it. The island, with its reputation as a hippy centre, was away from the mainland of Francoist Spain and could provide an attractive backdrop for designers of all nations to unite. For the conference an Instant City was created, along the lines that the radical British design group, Archigram, had proposed in 1969. Carles Ferrater described it in the national daily, *La Vanguardia*, as 'the first experience in this country in which one has attempted to consider construction as an expressive experience of human relations'. The Instant City was accompanied by a vast inflatable sculpture by Josep Ponsati and an opening ceremony including garishly coloured food organized by Antoni Miralda.

The ICSID conference was not only important in placing Spanish designers alongside foreign designers; it was also an ambitious expression of creativity that demonstrated an energetic interplay of design and artistic forces. The Instant City had been planned by the Grupo Abierto. This coalition of young photographers, artists, architects and designers included Pepe Cortés, Carles Ferrater and Ponsati. They were the only multi-disciplinary group in Spain at that time, and their work was brought back to Barcelona in the form of FAD's annual stand at the Hogarotel hotel and catering trade fair of the same year. The stand, which was housed in an inflatable, was divided into two rooms, joined by a long band of colour. The first included inflatable toys and a tape-slide installation which presented themes developed by ADIFAD such as industry, consumption, alienation and the future. The second room consisted of an exhibition of 63 objects selected by ADIFAD as examples of 'good design'. Thus the stand was both eminently cultural and clearly professional. One was to be invited in, challenged conceptually, before passing to consider objects, with new ideas in mind.

To a non-south European sensibility, this stand may appear to represent a schizophrenic conception of design. The first room is an ebullient, provocative and truly cultural expression of an experimental atmosphere, informed by the legacy of hippydom, happenings and conceptual art. The second is a sober professional demonstration of 'good design', continuing the moralistic traditions of Councils for Design. One might see this as the expression of the two platforms of design history: the first resting on the *ad hoc* level of groups, at times deriving from – but separate from – the second, that of the official institution ADIFAD. At times the coincidence of the two was problematic. Jaume

Lores, writing in the recently founded, progressive, Barcelona-based magazine *CAU* at the beginning of 1972, asked: 'Is *Made in Catalonia 1971* design a profession or a cultural movement?'. He suggested that: 'One could sum up the brief local history of design as being the misfortunes of a cultural movement that ended up opening a *boutique*.' Lores was concerned that the cultural approach to design would ultimately be unable to consolidate itself in Spanish industry.

These two differing aspects of design co-existed happily through the 1970s. Out of the enthusiastic activities undertaken in 1971, the Barcelona Centre de Disseny was founded, with the aim of promoting design in industry. Backed by the Barcelona Chamber of Commerce, the BCD was able to install an inflatable in the city's major street, the Diagonal, which was to house a permanent exhibition of 'good design'. Funding from the Chamber of Commerce was skilfully negotiated by Jordi Pujol, who was then director of the Banca Catalana and later to become president of the Autonomous Regional Government of Catalonia thoughout the 1980s – it is noteworthy that such funding could only come from an anti-centralist body: the Banca Catalana was the only Spanish bank at the time that did not have any strings attached to Madrid.

Inflatable to house the Barcelona Centre de Disseny in the Diagonal from 1973 to 1976.

In addition to its permanent exhibition, its centre of documentation, and seminars and courses on various aspects of the practice of design, the BCD also mounted exhibitions, such as Jordi Pablo's 'Un llenguatge amb objectes i formas' (a language with objects and forms) in 1976. This exhibition attempted – as one of its organizers, Mai Felip, reflected – 'to counter the conception of some of the design schools, which were very Bauhaus, and to move towards a language of objects which was more Mediterranean, more "us"'. It was didactic, encouraging the reconsideration of objects, even suggesting the possibility of an indigenous identity and significance of the object. Thus whilst the primary concern was the constant battle to convince industrialists of the need for design, there were also moments of pure non-commercial avant-gardism. Similar moves took place in the furniture shop Vinçon during this period: items for sale at the front of the shop, installations and happenings in the gallery space to be found at the back.

That such activities (which one might associate with the radical movements in design of the 1960s in other countries) were prolonged through the 1970s in Spain is symptomatic of *desfase*. *Desfase* existed both between Spain and other Western countries, and also within Spain between the cultural sphere and the political and economic spheres. The former may simply be explained by Spain's isolation from Europe and America, the latter by the fact that whilst Spain was plunged into economic crisis from 1973, the demise of Francoism created a rejuvenation of attitudes connected with cultural freedom, experimentation and growth, whereas in America and Europe, 'the dream had already ended'.

The economic miracle of the development years came to a sudden end in 1973. Economic growth figures had been skewered upwards only partially by industry – the other important aspect was the huge invisible earnings made by the thousands of Spaniards working abroad and sending money back home and also by the tourist boom. The oil crisis of 1973 and the following world economic depression meant the end of a liberal attitude towards foreign workers in countries such as Switzerland and Germany, and also a drop in tourism to Spain. Furthermore, Spain was heavily reliant on imported oil and the rise in the price of oil precipitated by the OPEC countries dealt a harsh blow to the economy.

At the same time, the level of anti-Francoist agitation was stepping up. This came from a wide spectrum of interests – from students in the wake of the international student unrest of 1968; from the Church, which until the 1960s had been a mainstay of the regime and now was experiencing a massive outflow of priests; from the middle-class intelligentsia which might align itself with all political colours and creeds; and from the clandestine, but highly influential Communist Party, which had about 22,000 members abroad, maintained a constant level of opposition and was a prime mover behind the setting up of the general workers' union, *Comisiones Obreras*, as an alternative to the government-controlled *sindicatos verticales*.

The death of Franco on 20 November 1975 was, for many, a much-celebrated event. Designer Josep Lluscà recalls how previously, in order to obtain banned books, he would drive from Barcelona up to Montpellier across the French border to buy them. After 1975, he was able to see as many as 12 once-censored foreign films in a weekend. In this context, the cultural initiatives undertaken by designers continued to expand with increasing euphoria. However, at the same time, the economic crisis gradually took its toll. By 1978, virtually all sponsorship for the BCD had dried up. Many companies were buckling under the pressure of the economic crisis, making it yet harder for the designer to get a leverage on industry.

After 36 years of Francoism, Spain had to find new forms of government and economic organization. In 1977 Spain reapplied for EEC membership and was accepted the following year, though a transitional period had to be allowed for the country to bring herself in line with EEC practices, such as the regularizing of state barriers and the establishment of patent laws. By the time it became a formal member at the beginning of 1986, the situation was clear. Spain was now more open to foreign investment and European trading benefits, and it was certain that the old trading barriers would have to go. By 1992, and the arrival of the Single European Market, Spain would have to fend for itself, competing at the same level with the Germans and the Italians. Products would have to reach international standards in quality and price.

The process of democratization was undertaken gradually through the late 1970s. A new constitution was approved by national referendum in 1978 and the previous year, in Spain's first General Election for forty years, the victor was the centrist Unión Centro Democrático. In 1982, following an unsteady period of government, the Partido Socialista Obrero Español, under Felipe González, won the General Election to establish a socialist government from Madrid which would remain throughout the 1980s.

Of great importance for the destiny of Spain was the decentralization of power. During the Francoist period, the *dictatura* had attempted to create a unified nation state, suppressing regional identities. Resistance to such suppression, in particular in Catalonia and the Basque Country, had been strong and in October 1979 central government approved autonomy for these two regions. The character of autonomy had strong resonances for the status of design.

The Statute of Autonomy retained power for the central government over economic policy in regard to monetary and economic cycles, foreign trade, the public sector of the state, labour policy and social security; the Regional Government was given exclusive power over housing, planning and public works, and extensive powers over economic development, agricultural policy and domestic trade. Thus it could be said that if the central government retained control of the macro-economic demand-side policy, the regional government had some control over the micro-economic supply side. In terms of design, this meant that while a regional government could not affect control on capital expenditure, it would intervene in a more direct way. Almost in opposition to centralist government, to mark out its own territory, a regional government would pay particular attention to the public image of the region, thus calling for wholesale re-designing of its transport systems, its public spaces and its corporate identity. Additionally, new education systems, civil service patterns and social services had to be devised and re-presented. Each new logo, each new park bench, each new street sign would symbolize a fresh start for the new Valencia, the new Madrid, the new Bilbao or Barcelona.

Both central and regional governments were involved in *reconversión industrial*. To confront the mandate for EEC entry, incentives and infrastructures had to be offered to industry to re-convert itself for the international market. The INI was to lose its potency in the Spanish economy. Henceforth, industries themselves would have to fend for themselves. Within this process, a few design-led companies, in particular those producing furniture, had already undertaken this step. Behind these companies there were methodologically solid designers who had 15 years experience in demanding and creating higher standards without needing guidance from above. Thus, while Spain's export figures in furniture represented a tiny percentage of the total, designers and design-led furniture manufacturers carried a high symbolic level for the new Spain. Indeed, in a rather propagandist article published in the short-lived magazine *El Globo* in September 1987, the designer Oscar Tusquets and the furniture manufacturer Txema García Amiano of Akaba were both invoked as being symptomatic of the Third Spain: not the poor agricultural Spain or the heavy-industry Spain, but a sector distanced from state supervision, relying on ingenuity and innovation. Furniture was also symbolic of the type of industry with which Spain might compete. Without vast resources in raw materials or in high technology, Spain could compete with consumer goods.

In 1986, the Spanish economy experienced an upturn. Bankruptcies and suspension of payments were the lowest in 1986 since 1977; foreign investment from EEC countries to Spain doubled between 1985 and 1986 and investment to EEC countries tripled; the Madrid share prices general index moved from about 75 points to about 200 points during 1986, having moved less than 50 points since mid-1983. Much work for designers had been provided by central government, regional governments and local councils. Now it looked that industry would take up this charge. The resultant growth in consumption meant that a domestic market, in particular for furniture, expanded. The Barcelona furniture shop, Vinçon, underwent its first expansion of floor space since 1972 in 1986. Also in 1986 Spanish furniture gained greater international recognition than ever before via the Milan Furniture Fair.

If design was about creating a new national identity, it was also about recovering lost traditions as well. In 1986 the Ministry of Industry and Energy sponsored an itinerant exhibition organized by the BCD, which was to promote the concept of design throughout Spain. Nearly two-thirds of the exhibition was taken up by historical precedents, demonstrating that Spain in fact had a long tradition in design. Part of this ideology was to act as a foil to the possible trivialization brought about by a design boom. It was considered – in particular by those who had been involved in design for many years – that whilst their battle cry was finally being taken up by the government, it was in danger of being used as an electoral tool. Which administration could out-design the other was at stake. (This was especially strong in Barcelona, where the centre-right regional government was matched by a socialist city council.) On the public level, it was feared that design would be seen as fashion rather than the intrinsic creation of a destiny. On a commercial level, designers and the designers' institutions took note that companies were very keen to change their image (thus creating much employment for graphic designers), but did not take the step of changing their identity (thus creating work for industrial designers).

This disjuncture between image and identity continued to bring up the problem endemic in the schizophrenic condition of Spanish design. At one level there

Calder lamp
Metal with halogen bulb and
dimmer
Enric Franch
Metalarte S.A.
Designed 1975
Responding to the pressures of the
economic crisis, Metalarte's
catalogue of lamps went through a
markedly conservative phase.
However, an avant-garde edge was
maintained by the production of
such examples as this. Still highly
successful in the 1990s, it
testifies to the fact that Spain's
design boom has deeper roots than
often reported.

was its cultural history: informal, submerged and renegade, associated with exclusive short-run furniture, design bars and events. At another level there existed its formal, more industrial state. These two states co-existed – but sometimes they also coincided, as in the work of a versatile designer such as Oscar Tusquets, or in a design such as Jorge Pensi's Toledo chair (1988), where personal investigation met mass production.

The successes of design in Spain during the 1980s most often lay where the historically constructed approaches of a sense of individualism combined with a versatile use of the language of design, free from any constraints of rigid design theologies. The significance of Spanish design was to be strengthened in relation to its historical background. Once ignored by government, it was now the darling of ministers and councillors. Always internationalist, it was to be appropriated for the national good.

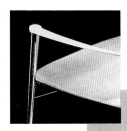

2

furniture

The Unification of Culture and Commerce

Left: Spinnacker chair
Walnut, with chrome and leather
edgings
Jaime Tresserra
J. Tresserra S.L.
1988

IT IS IN FURNITURE THAT SPANISH DESIGN has achieved greatest recognition; in terms of export figures, it has been the most successful design area. Some of the reasons are obvious: interior design or graphic design is difficult to export, while the possibilities for expression in furniture are also greater than for product design. Furniture has been made emblematic, and thus exportable. Moreover, the overall development of design in Spain has also favoured furniture over other design disciplines.

Just as the development of design in its global definition was to be found in the art, design and architecture colleges of Barcelona in the 1960s and the design institutes of FAD and the BCD, the development of modern single-piece furniture in Spain is also due to a localized handful of individuals in Barcelona. These include the proprietor of Vinçon, Fernando Amat; the designers and also proprietors of Gris, Bigas Luna and Carlos Riart; the furniture manufacturer Carlos Riera, who ran Disform; and the members of Studio Per, Oscar Tusquets, Lluís Clotet, Pep Bonet and Cristian Cirici, who founded B.D. Ediciones de Diseño and the furniture company Casas/Mobilplast.

From the 1960s Spain's major showcase of modern furniture was a shop called Vinçon, situated in the Passeig de Gràcia in Barcelona, next to Gaudí's La Pedrera. Its director, Fernando Amat (b.1941), was neither a designer nor a manufacturer. His interest lay entirely in a love of the object, and buying and selling it. His father, Jacinto, had run the shop since 1940, dedicating it to the import and sale of fine German porcelain. Under Fernando's directorship it moved into gifts, office and shop equipment and also included an exhibition room. In 1967, however, following a period of dissatisfaction with what it had been selling, Vinçon took the conscious step of giving priority to products that Amat preferred, rather than what the market appeared to demand. From this point onwards, the direction of Vinçon was to be blantantly avant-garde.

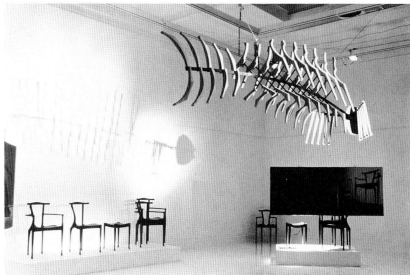

Above left: Vinçon, in the Passeig de Gràcia, Barcelona.

Above right: Installation for the presentation of Oscar Tusquets's Gaulino chair in La Sala Vinçon, 1987.

In this respect, Vinçon's most important model was Britain's Habitat stores. (Indeed, in 1974, Fernando Amat, through his friends, Charles and Jane Dillon, went to meet Terence Conran in London, though Amat was so overcome by the excitement of the visit that any possibility of 'joint ventures' was not discussed.) The important difference from Habitat was that Vinçon remained a single shop, rather than expanding into a chain of stores. Thereby Amat kept control of the stock and presentation of the shop – he recognized that any change, even in the interior layout, meant that the overall concept of the shop had to be reconsidered. To view the shop itself as an evolving object of design was fundamental.

Fernando Amat consistently maintained close contact with Barcelona's artistic and designerly avant-garde. In fact for a period in the late 1960s and early 1970s he shared a house in Arenys with Bigas Luna (with whom he later co-directed the film *Bilbao*) and Toni Mirò. La Sala Vinçon, the shop's exhibition hall, was re-opened in 1973, and acted as a platform for discourse on the everyday object, with installations, performance and, of course, conceptual art. Its first exhibition in March 1973 was of Bigas Luna's eminently Postmodern tables, which questioned and subverted the language of furniture. Since these earlier days, Fernando Amat has remained a great *animateur* of design. Rarely getting involved at any official level, he has promoted work either via Vinçon's gallery or by his encouragement to other producers and designers to develop projects. Indeed, in tracing the network of contacts between producers and designers, all paths seem to lead past Amat's door. By the close of the 1980s, Terence Conran was looking interestedly towards Vinçon.

Posters celebrating the first 100 exhibitions of the La Sala Vinçon, 1988.

'Taules' by Bigas Luna, 1973, exhibited in La Sala Vinçon. In 1975 these tables were exhibited at the Art Net Gallery, London through Bigas Luna's friendship with members of Archigram. The catalogue of this exhibition was introduced by Alessandro Mendini.

For his part, Bigas Luna, together with his friend, Carlos Riart, had run since 1968 a small interior decor shop in Barcelona called Gris. Again, this shop *created* a demand through exhibiting radically modern objects such as Charles and Jane Dillon's Kite lamp (Bigas Luna first met them in 1971 when he went to London to learn English).

Carlos Riart began training as an industrial technician, but soon left – aged 19 – to work with Bigas Luna. He spent a brief period as a student at Eina in 1967 in order 'to find out what the world of design was all about.' Importantly, he also undertook an apprenticeship in a cabinetmaker's workshop. He was thus equipped to be a designer-maker.

A trip to London and to Charles and Jane Dillon's studio in 1974 was influential, for (like Bigas Luna) he found in them kindred spirits. They were producing designer-maker furniture with the dual aims of being accessible (cheaper) and also provocative (objects with references, conceits, distortions, etc.). He and Bigas Luna sold Gris and, with the money from it, Luna bought equipment to make films (which he has done ever since), but Riart set up a workshop to make his own furniture. His first production was a flatpack panel-system wardrobe which he tried, unsuccessfully, to sell from a stall outside Barcelona football stadium on match days. He also designed (1976) and made the Colilla lighting system, which he sold by mail order. This lamp was designed to warm rather than light spaces, and consisted of a row of neon bulbs inside a translucent tube.

This lamp formed part of a 1976 exhibition which found much greater success than his wardrobe venture. The exhibition, at the furniture shop Tecmo, consisted of pieces which were often subsequently described as 'Memphis before Memphis'. (Carlos Riart sent photographs to Alessandro Mendini, which he sent back without showing interest. News of it wasn't published in the Italian magazine *Modo* until 1980.) It included pyramidal bookshelves, a multi-coloured chair and pieces of undefined function. Whilst Riart claimed the direction he took here came merely 'from personal interest and need', the collection possessed all the eclecticism and referential and functional ambiguity that was to emerge in Italy five years later. In the early 1970s, Ettore Sottsass was a frequent visitor to Barcelona (he had a girlfriend there) and there were informal links kept with designers, including Riart. Still Riart's 'Memphis before Memphis' might best be seen as a parallel line, born of the same *inquietud*.

Carlos Riart's designs were very rarely produced in long runs. Even during the late 1980s, when other producers were extending the production of designs, Riart installed himself in the workshops of Casas, where he produced with a cut-down team of fourteen craftsmen many of his designs of the 1970s to order. For Riart, this was continuing his Morrisite ideal, which to him answered both personal and political needs. Yet if his work was not as ubiquitous as other designers, his influence was profound at the level of the individualistic treatment applied to each project, and in demonstrating to other designers the possibilities of expression that were available to furniture designers.

Possibly the only Spanish designer to follow Riart's line of high-quality cabinet-making is Jaime Tresserra. After a varied career, starting as a silver-smith, moving rapidly through publicity to interior design and architecture before settling on furniture design, he eventually established a company to produce his own furniture designs in 1986. Having travelled to several furniture fairs, Tresserra observed that there were no Spanish producers offering pieces to the top end of the market. To produce his designs, he set up a workshop of twenty cabinet-makers. Nearly all of his craftsmen were aged over 55. This may explain why there was no one else producing for his chosen audience. Barcelona's reputation for high-standard craftsmanship had become based more on myth than reality; the demand for such work had dropped during the Francoist era and particularly during the economic crisis of the 1970s. Tresserra produced an astonishingly large catalogue of pieces in the first three years, each new piece becoming more provocative and daring than the last. This activity was rewarded by several accolades, including the featuring of some of his furniture in the 1989 film *Batman*. Furthermore, unlike much Spanish design, his work found its strongest market in Britain, where Tresserra presumed, 'there still exists a demand for high standard wood-working'.

It was in the middle range that most of the pioneering work in modern furniture production was carried out in Barcelona. Miguel Milà had demonstrated with the TMC lamp in 1957 that there did exist the industrial resources to produce modern designs in the form of semi-artisanal workshops through which one could produce in small batches. During the 1960s several initiatives continued to produce modern designs. These included Metalarte, a lamp producer that was able to take advantage of the consumer boom which accompanied the economic miracle of that decade to develop a modern line alongside their more traditional brass-turned lamps. Other pioneers were Casas Mobilplast, an offspring of the Casas furniture makers already mentioned. From 1961, Casas Mobilplast produced foreign designs under licence, subsequently developing their own collection from 1978. They began by introducing furniture of expanded polystyrene from Norway, and in 1968 introduced polyurethane technology via an agreement with C & B of Novedrate (B & B Italy). Subsequent negotiation and inter-marriage between the families of Casas and Cassina consolidated international links. Casas/Mobilplast was developed firstly for cultural reasons (breaking from traditional patterns in Spanish furniture and its commercialization), secondly as a technological investigation (exploring materials and processes otherwise untouched in Spain), thirdly as an internationalizing activity (bringing in foreign designers or exporting products) – and lastly as a money-making venture. This was a common order of priorities amongst producers during these early years.

Design-led editing companies were not consolidated until the 1970s. One of the pioneers was Carlos Riera, director of Disform. The Riera family were the proprietors of the lighting company, Metalarte; in late 1969, however, Carlos set up on his own to produce and distribute other domestic objects.

Editing has distinct advantages over centralized production for design-led companies. Drawing on the many (but not necessarily highly skilled), almost garage-sized artisanal workshops in Barcelona, the producer was able to farm out each separate stage of the production process to a different, specialist workshop. Subsequently, the assemblage of parts (not often complicated in furniture and lighting) would take place on the limited premises of the producer/distributor. Disform itself used four metals workshops and two woodworking shops, assembling the pieces in the company's factory space in St Just Desvern.

The major advantage of this system is that the initial investment needed on the part of the editor is little, since he doesn't need his own factory space and machinery. Without the risk factor of high investment in tooling, the editor is therefore free to place his risk elsewhere, in the product itself, and furthermore, runs on products may be lengthened or shortened easily, according to demand. The editor's major problem is in keeping quality control over a range of workshops that might be widely dispersed, both geographically and in their specialisms. Whilst the editor of modern furniture demanded much higher standards of

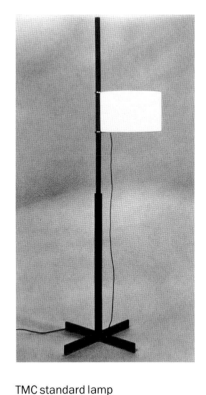

TMC standard lamp
Miguel Milà
Polinax S.A.
1961
Various versions of this lamp were produced by Polinax, Maenfra-Tramo, B.D. Ediciones de Diseño and Santa & Cole for more than twenty years. As such, it became something of a 'classic' of modern Spanish design.

production, and sometimes more technologically sophisticated products, there never existed in Spain the apparatus for developing editing networks along the lines of the 'high-tech cottage industry' phenomenon that was found in northern Italy in the 1970s. With a few exceptions (which we shall look at later on), this parameter has shaped Spanish furniture design by imposing more emphasis on the aesthetic rather than the technological end of production.

Unlike its forebears, Disform's catalogue was to be exclusively of modern design (the name, Disform, is itself a contraction of Diseño y Forma – design and form). During the economic crisis of the 1970s, Metalarte's catalogues became more conservative, not returning to any marked inclusion of avant-garde design until 1983-84. Meanwhile, Disform, with the much lower risk factor in investment, weathered the crisis with a solid and growing avant-garde catalogue. Starting off by editing a table-calender by Carlos Riart and Bigas Luna, a wastepaper bin by Alberto Udaeta and a seat by Cristianni, as well as importing the famous Alessi clocks of Colombo, Pio Manzú and Sapper, Disform passed via editing Charles and Jane Dillon's Cometa light in 1972 to editing its first pieces of furniture from 1977. Over half of Disform's designs were by non-Spanish designers, thus bringing in new forms, new ideas and new demands. Among those included was the then (1983) unrecognized Parisian designer, Philippe Starck, who was unable himself to find the time to produce his own designs because of his commitments in interior design. The objects therefore did not necessarily conform to any national design characteristic – rather, to the company's own product philosophy: this included an unsophisticated technological level, an emphasis on being easily understood, simple construction and longevity. Philippe Starck's Jon Ild shelving was a good example. This tendency towards simplicity was as much a result of the market as of the lack of sophisticated materials in Spain: for lacquers and materials such as medium-density fibre-board, Riera would have to go to Italy.

Another important aspect of Disform's catalogue was that it was of kit furniture. In the rest of Europe this was not a new concept. In Spain it represented a whole new way of seeing. Without exposure to the historical precedents of, say, the pack-down furniture of Rietveld, the re-working of furniture under Gordon Russell in Utility Britain of the Second World War, or the development of Scandinavian kit furniture during the 1940s, the possibility of radically rethinking furniture in Spain had largely gone unnoticed. Kit furniture could be easily exported in varying numbers (single pieces could even be posted) and also suggested new possibilities in jointing, hinging and decorative detailing and in effect for a different aesthetic.

As well as importing many significant designs and designers onto the Spanish market, Disform was instrumental in the growing export of Spanish furniture.

In 1982, Carlos Riera exhibited at the Milan Furniture Fair with B.D. Ediciones de Diseño, sharing a stand 5 metres by 5 metres. In 1984 he returned with a much bigger and more successful stand, establishing Disform definitively on the international market – 30-36 per cent of its sales by 1988, 50 per cent by 1990.

Thus Carlos Riera's contribution to the rise of new Spanish furniture has been in several directions: in bringing foreign designers to the Spanish market; in proving the viability of a design-led policy; in developing the editing of new furniture; and in consolidating Spanish furniture in the international market.

Like Fernando Amat, Carlos Riera has never himself trained as a designer, though he has always been closely connected with designers. Indeed, he even attended the 1971 ICSID Ibiza conference, where he 'didn't understand much of it, but had a great time'. Some other editing companies established in the 1970s were created by designers themselves. Of these perhaps the most important has been B.D. Ediciones de Diseño.

The ventures of Gris and Vinçon had clearly demonstrated that a market existed for modern design. At the same time, few manufacturers apart from those already mentioned were willing to tackle the concept themselves. B.D. was put into action to edit objects by a group of architects and designers who otherwise would not have found interested manufacturers.

At the core of the creation of B.D. in 1972 were members of Studio Per, Oscar Tusquets, Lluís Clotet, Pep Bonet and Cristian Cirici. All four came from the almost statutory progressive middle-class family backgrounds and studied architecture together at the Escuela Técnica y Superior de Arquitectura de Barcelona, graduating in 1965 to set up Studio Per. As students, Tusquets and Clotet worked in the studio of Correa-Milà, working on the interiors of their many *chic* Costa Brava holiday homes. Thus like other compatriots of the later Escuela de Barcelona, they had worked across from architecture to interiors to industrial design. Studio Per represented the younger, more restless generation of the Escuela de Barcelona. Indeed, in an article published in 1969, Alexandre Cirici identified them with the generation of the 1960s, who did their bacca-lauréat with the Sputnik, who entered university with Fidel Castro, and had passed through youth with the Beatles, Pop Art and the mini-skirt, and, 'are incorporating themselves into active life at the moment of the consumer boom, of the sexual revolution and the youth movements of Paris, Amsterdam and Berkeley'. 'Amongst the architects', he wrote, 'is the Postmodern attitude, with its marked hedonism, from the accurate design of Lluís Domènech, to the Studio Per.... and to the *adhoc* fantastical and capricious irrationalism of Ricardo Bofill.'

The incorporation of a 'Postmodern attitude' was an alignment with internat-ional movements: Oscar Tusquets's family publishing house, Tusquets Editores, was responsible for bringing out a Spanish edition of Robert Venturi's *Learning from Las Vegas* in 1972. It was also a response to local conditions: as we have seen in the first chapter, by the late 1960s, it was no longer avant-garde to take up an exclusively Modernist position. What had been Modernist was not sufficiently appropriated by Francoism to lose its oppositional character. Together with the input of marginalized architects and designers, the avant-garde agenda was now set on the small, individualistic scale where subversion and irony of pre-existing languages were *de rigueur*.

The design of Studio Per, and more specifically of Oscar Tusquets and Lluís Clotet, is thus fragmentary and eclectic whilst maintaining an architect's precision. Tusquets's most absorbing passion was as a painter: his canvases demonstrate a Vermeeresque fastidiousness and absorption with depicting everyday objects and interiors (in Tusquets's case, light bulbs and fridges). This demanding approach is carried through to his design work, for instance in the detailing of the Hypóstila shelving system (1980), or the proportioning of the Tea or Coffee Piazza (1980) for Alessi.

Gaulino chair
Oak with leather seat
Oscar Tusquets
Carlos Jané S.A.
Designed 1986

At the same time, Tusquets and Clotet kept an open book on influences. Some of their design work from the early 1970s, such as their Cuc lamp, reflects an interest in conceptual art. In 1980 they took part in the Design Forum exhibition in Linz, which set out to define various concepts of design according to different approaches – commercial, historical, individual and thematic. Clotet and Tusquets, along with others such as Sottsass, Pentagram and Raymond Loewy, submitted their own reflection on design as an installation and answered the question: 'What Can I Enjoy For 10 Pesetas A Day?' Thus they presented one eighth of a cow, two and a half cigarettes, two square metres of house, and so on. they drew attention to objects as functions of value, cutting across pre-conceptions of the purpose of design with an economic scythe.

Not all their work is charged with such irony and sarcasm. However, their distrust of dogma made them more open to explore a variety of visual languages. Thus Tusquets's Varius chair (1984) for Casas/Mobilplast was inspired by the shape of a violin – hence its name, derived from Stradivarius. Similarly, in the Gaulino chair (1986) he combines aspects of both Gaudí and the 1940s Italian designer, Carlo Mollino. In the Banco Catalano, Tusquets and Clotet appear to recall the profile of Gaudí's seats for the Parque Guell. These are conscious quotations. At other times, his designs may be accused of being derivative: Tusquets's urban seating for Hijo de E. F. Escofet in 1988, the Sofanco, recalls the French designer, Pierre Paulin's seating of 1965. For Tusquets these influences are not just a form of learning, but a vehicle to subvert, to improve or to give inflexions. Perhaps his success stems partly from both the evocative and provocative qualities of his work.

Certainly his success also depends on his character. Unlike, for instance, Carlos Riart, Oscar Tusquets is a master of his own publicity. Like Salvador Dalí, with whom he had a long friendship, Tusquets was inclined to be the *provocateur*. He has also had the breaks. Firstly, as Cirici noted in the late 1960s, he was part of a particular generation that rode the wave of the political and cultural changes from 1965. Secondly, as an architect he was well connected to other members of the avant-garde in Barcelona and internationally. In Barcelona, this came through his association with members of the Escuela de Barcelona and the *kudos* of architecture as a university subject. And internationally, alongside Bofill, he came to be seen by Charles Jencks as the representative of Postmodern architecture in Spain. It was with the Tea and Coffee set for Alessi, part of their architects' designing tea sets series in 1980, that Tusquets received his most significant international launch. His particular set is the only one that remained in production through the 1980s. These pieces of good fortune were accompanied by a fastidiousness behind each project and a keen anti-intellectualism. In 1985 his association with Lluís Clotet ended, replaced by an architectural studio with Carlos Diaz, which was set up to deal with more complex architectural projects (leaving to Diaz the more bureaucratic end of these projects, which Tusquets himself hated). Tusquets was also largely able to remove himself from the designerly euphoria of Spain in the late-1980s to concentrate on perfecting basic problems in design. His designs increasingly benefited from the time and energy concentrated on them, rather than on their justification.

Meanwhile, as B.D. developed, it diversified both in the kind of furniture sold and the production process. Its showroom was broader than any Milan showroom, importing both historical re-editions (Aalto, Hoffmann, Mackintosh) and recent pieces (du Pasquier, Scarpa, Sapper). Its production similarly ran from artisanal suppliers in the re-edition of Gaudí and Domènech i Muntaner furniture, to the highly mechanized in the production of the Banco Catalano or the Hialina shelving. Whilst Vinçon never expanded and was never directly involved in production, B.D. consistently took the cream of the national market, importing, producing or distributing.

The successes of such shops as Gris, Vinçon, B.D. and Pilma in Barcelona had shown that modern furniture had a domestic market. Furthermore, producers

Oronda tea set
Silver plate
Oscar Tusquets
Alessi
1980
Alessandro Mendini once commented to Tusquets: 'You've made yourself one of the eleven best architects in the world by making a tea set.'

B.D. Ediciones de Diseño,
Barcelona, housed in Lluís
Domènech i Montaner's Casa
Thomas of 1898.

such as B.D., Perobell, Disform, Casas/Mobilplast, Grupo T and 114 Mobles had demonstrated their strengths in marketing and technical questions, thus placing them in a wider national and international market. Yet their efforts were dissipated both by the sporadic nature of their individual appearances at international furniture fairs and the lack of international recognition that Spanish design received. The Salón Internacional de Diseño del Equipamiento para el Habitat (SIDI) was to rectify this problem.

In 1978 Carme Llopis and Carme Ferrer founded in Barcelona Spain's first exclusively design magazine, called *On* (meaning 'where' in Catalan). Its editorial line was rigorous in representing problems and debates in design in Spain, whilst at the same time featuring the latest developments in design. The result, however, was to highlight inherited problems in the commercialization of design. Llopis and Ferrer therefore formed SIDI in 1983 to act as an umbrella organization for furniture manufacturers, funded by member companies and central government. Membership was open to producers of designer articles. Otherwise, SIDI was an open platform through which the concept of Spanish furniture design would be consolidated, particularly through the furniture fairs. Its first appearance was in September 1984, at the Valencia Furniture Fair, this being the leading show of its kind in Spain. Here, 30 firms took part under the SIDI banner, and after its success SIDI was invited to take part in the Paris Furniture Fair the following January. Soon, in the September 1986 Milan Furniture Fair, Spanish furniture design was to receive probably its most unanimously enthusiastic acclaim, after showing that interesting pieces were available at extremely competitive prices. Thus SIDI rapidly established itself at both national and international levels. In offering an accessible platform for companies, it encouraged them to place themselves on the international agenda. Given this exposure, companies had to learn to play the international market very quickly.

Producers responded to the rapidly expanding national and international position in varying ways. The editing company Santa & Cole was launched with a show at Vinçon in 1986. Its founders were brothers-in-law Gabriel Ordeig, a painter, interior designer and former rock-band promoter, and Javier Nieto, a frustrated philosopher and former economist and publisher. They bought up a factory space that was formerly a building in the 1929 Barcelona Exhibition, by an unknown but possibly Austrian architect. This acted as their assembly space and later their showroom. The idiosyncrasy of the building – almost an Expressionist hanger, with sweeping arched beams, transported from the exhibition site to the hills above Barcelona, and renovated according to Gabriel Ordeig's design – is a fitting metaphor for the commercial style of Santa & Cole. Within two years of opening, their capital had risen from three million pesetas (invested, typically, out of the founders' own pockets) to three times that amount; by 1989

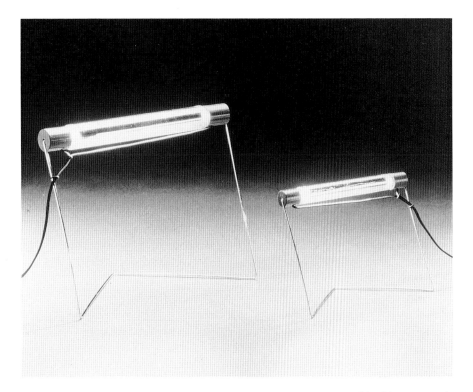

Lamparaprima
Chromium-plated iron structure,
with translucent tubular bulb
Pete Sans
Santa & Cole S.A.
Designed 1979

they were opening ten more showrooms throughout Spain, and had become sole distributors of the highly acclaimed German kitchen systems manufactured by Bulthaup. Of course, acting as editors, Santa & Cole were able to function effectively on such a low initial investment. Moreover, many of their initial projects were re-editions which allowed a large and varied catalogue to be established rapidly.

Among these re-editions were Angel Jové and Santiago Roqueta's alabaster Zeleste lamps, which were originally created in 1968 for the bar of the same name (see pp. 132, 134). They were designed in homage to Ettore Sottsass, who was a frequenter of the bar at that time. Their disquieting and even neo-kitsch quality, as well as the association they held with the popular bar, meant that they maintained an emblematic presence through to their 1986 re-edition. Angel Jové was well known on Barcelona's avant-garde circuit as a novelist, painter, film-writer and actor (indeed, he took leading parts in Bigas Luna's *Bilbao, Caniche* and *Anguish*). Likewise, Santiago Roqueta was also known as an architect, interior designer and cultural *animateur*. Other re-editions included Carlos Riart's Colilla lamp (1976) and Pete Sans's Lamparaprima (1979), which had already won an impressive string of national and international design prizes.

Thus from the start, while these examples were highly acceptable designs in their own right, Santa & Cole were also involved in recuperation of an avant-garde, extending and consolidating the life of designs which were not yet loaded with the resonances of history, and yet carried 'known' associations.

Santa & Cole took this one step further in 1990 by launching a Classic Spanish line, in which they published lost classic designs by Coderch or Jujol with a book including technical drawings and the history of the designer. Their previous catalogues had already shown an often criticized propensity for accompanying the object with plenty of text; and this leaning towards reflection, and even philosophizing, on their own progress and context, acted as a foil to their own success. As well as re-editions, their catalogue had technically unsophisticated, yet noticeable pieces, many by younger designers. This noticeability in turn publicized their work and thus allowed a rapid expansion. In the face of their own and the general design boom, with all its potentially misplaced euphoria, Santa & Cole played down their own designerism, expecting to consolidate their progress by a constant process of reflection on it.

Santa & Cole's search for classics to strengthen their position may be contrasted with Akaba's relentless avant-gardism. Akaba was launched in 1983 in San Sebastián and its founder, Txema García Amiano, had previously worked with Enea. However, whilst Enea's industrial reconversion in the early 1980s was very much technology, rather than product-dominated, García Amiano was more interested in furniture as a form of creative investigation. Furniture would then become an accessible art: not a startlingly original idea of the twentieth century, but none the less still legitimate. Deeply critical of the way of which he saw the Italian producers, such as Cassina and Zanotta, lose their progressive edge as their fame and sales grew, he wanted Akaba to be more like it was in the 1950s, taking risks with young designers, but still dominated by the idea of a homogeneous collection rather than a disparate coalition of designs. Meanwhile, being at a respectful distance from Barcelona meant that Akaba would not get sucked into any of its 'mannerisms', though many of its designers in fact came from or near Barcelona. One example was Ramón Benedito, who, together with his design group, Transatlántic, was better known as a product designer of Ulm-school inspiration; with Akaba, they were able to 'let off steam' with the precarious form of the Frenesi stool (1984).

When Fernando Amat introduced García Amiano to Mariscal in 1984, Akaba was barely off the ground. For his part, Mariscal had done some projects with B.D. Ediciones de Diseño and taken part with, for example, Michele de Lucchi and Ettore Sottsass in the Memphis adventure of 1981 in Milan, though this had already passed out of the design magazines. Mariscal's angular graphic work had been in evidence since the mid-1970s. He worked fast, with little prelimin-

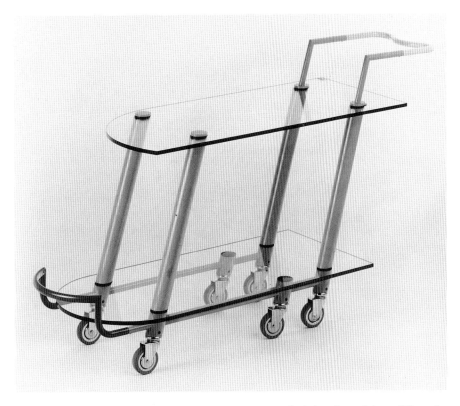

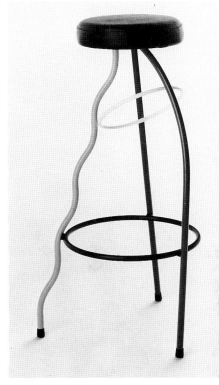

ary investigation, working off a direct, intuitive feel for the subject. When he came to design a stool for the Duplex Bar in Valencia in 1980, his long-time friend and 'technical brain', Pepe Cortés, took him to a small workshop, where a metalworker produced its rickety legs in a matter of minutes. 'Heavens, this furniture-making business is a piece of cake', he later exclaimed about it in an interview published in *Barcelona Diseño*. There will be many who disagree, but it remains true that Mariscal's hands-on, sketchy approach turned furniture into *fun*iture in Spain. His racy trolley for the Memphis show and his Muebles Amorales for the Sala Vinçon, both in 1981, demonstrated an irreverence for domestic convention. His *Muebles muy Formales* (1983), designed with Pepe Cortés for B.D., continued a 1950s bent-coathanger feel.

Mariscal designed pieces for Akaba which were to be exhibited in Paris in 1987 in the Pompidou Centre exhibition, 'Nouvelles Tendances', and mark Akaba's style in the national and international arena. His first pieces for Akaba, such as the Trampolín chair (1986), were eccentric sketches in the air made possible, once again, by Pepe Cortés, and his work shown in Paris invoked some of his cartoon characters. Akaba's furniture was seen by some as frivolous, a

Above left: Hilton trolley
Glass and painted iron
Javier Mariscal, with Pepe Cortés
Memphis, Milan
1981

Above right: Duplex stool
Painted tubular steel and leather seat
Javier Mariscal, with Pepe Cortés
B.D. Ediciones de Diseño
Designed 1980
The Duplex stool was designed for the bar of the same name.
Subsequently, Mariscal took part in the Memphis group in Milan, his offering being the Hilton trolley.

Araña lamp
Steel wire legs with anodized
aluminium shade
Pepe Cortés and Javier Mariscal
B.D. Ediciones de Diseño
1983
This lamp formed part of the
designers' exhibition at B.D.,
Muebles muy Formales (very
formal furniture). Previous
exhibitions included *Muebles
Amorales* (amoral furniture) in
1980 (La Sala Vinçon) and
*Esculturas adelantadas en el
nuevo estilo Post-Barocco*
(sculptures 'jazzed up' in the new
Post-Baroque style) in 1986 (La
Sala Vinçon).

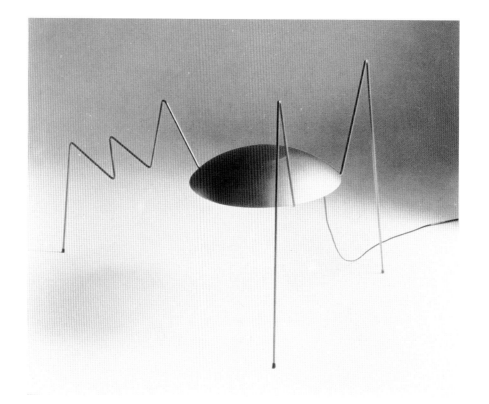

criticism that Txema García Amiano countered by pointing out that he also ran a design management consultancy, and was well aware of different solutions for different problems. Thus Akaba's complete catalogue pushed the boundaries of furniture further, dealing with the problems brought about by any design boom by attempting to stride ahead of it, building rather than changing their range every year. Mariscal's fame as a comic drawer, graphic designer and unintentional *provocateur*, as well as breakthroughs in the international arena (to be discussed in greater detail in Chapter 3), no doubt helped Akaba consolidate its line, which was consistent in itself, but unlike any other Spanish furniture company. Its wackiness was regarded by many as the most Postmodern Spanish offering, an epithet based heavily on a Memphis-experience perception of what 'Postmodern' meant. Those who called it thus did not like it, and those who were called it did not necessarily enjoy the title.

Other furniture companies in the 1980s produced individual pieces which were to be emblematic crowd-pullers and strong designs in their own right, but not necessarily representative of their entire catalogues. This erratic, though effective behaviour was no doubt a response to the growing interest in new design and its widening media coverage. Produce a noticeable design and buyers will remember your name. This became increasingly manifest at trade fairs; for instance, at the Valencia Furniture Fair of 1989, Chueca, S.A., who normally produce middle-of-the-road glass-top tables, had pushed some extraordinary furniture by Antoni Riera, reminiscent of Tusquets and Tresserra but in glass, to the front of their stand. At times talented young designers such as the Valencian, Juan Ramón Ferrandis, found themselves having to create lines in designerly modern-kitsch for companies anxious to prove their Postmodern worth. In the 1950s and 1960s, architects of the Escuela de Barcelona had reacted against the corporate modernism which had turned into a kitsch parody of itself. It seemed that by the 1980s such problems in design had come full circle.

In bringing out 'instant classics', or at least marking out a producer's technological and/or aesthetic territory with emblematic projects, other companies with more experience in commericalizing modern design came up with more successful results than the ones we have just seen.

The most startling of these was Jorge Pensi's Toledo chair, brought out by Amat in 1988. This chair was designed for exteriors, being made entirely of moulded aluminium. Given the cost of developing moulds and the material (its initial retail price was 29,000 pesetas, or approximately £145/US $240), its commercialization represented a risk on the part of the manufacturer. It was a risk that paid off: the chair won a series of design prizes, gained much media coverage and, above all, it sold very well. It would grace the terraces of many new design bars throughout Spain, and also began to be used in interiors, too.

Nelly Schnaith, writing about it in *Ardi*, reclaimed it as a distinctly Mediterranean object, with its mixture of ostentatious play on light and an austerity in colour and form. Certainly the pierced aluminium seat and backrest allowed infinite combinations of light and shadow to work on it, whilst its form might have echoed everyday metal forms such as those found in train interiors, bar fittings or already existing terrace chairs. Pensi, however, took the terrace seat a step further. In Spain, terrace chairs were either of tubular steel frame with wooden or cane slats, or of moulded plastic. The exception to this was Indecasa's ubiquitous chair with aluminium frame and riveted slats, the slats being a translation from originally wooden ones. A chair entirely of moulded aluminium represented a bold new departure. At the same time, in keeping a weight/strength balance in order to keep costs down, the Toledo ended up with its distinctive slender proportions and ribbed form.

Jorge Pensi came to Barcelona from Buenos Aires in 1977 with his colleague Alberto Liévore. (They were among many Argentinians, including other designers such as Carlos Rolando, América Sánchez and J. García Garay, who from 1968 came to the liberal atmosphere of Barcelona, escaping the cultural and political stringencies of Argentina under an aggressive dictatorship.) After having studied architecture, Pensi and Liévore, together with the critics and theorists, Oriol Pibernat and Norberto Chaves, formed Grupo Berenguer to work on multi-disciplinary projects, including the stands for SIDI in 1984. Their strength lay in rigorous attitude and flexibility, thus offering a solid design package to interested clients. An important client was Perobell, a furniture company which converted to a co-operative in 1978, re-thinking its direction and presentation at the same time. In the early 1980s it launched its Latina range, with a re-design of corporate image and furniture by Pensi and Lievore which was to place Perobell on the international market both in terms of technological and aesthetic standards.

From 1984, Pensi and Liévore largely worked separately. Pensi, like Oscar Tusquets, worked on his own, perfecting furniture and lighting projects. Meanwhile, Alberto Liévore moved in the direction of objects of mass consumption, such as packaging and sanitary equipment, for he became increasingly frustrated with the growing 'frivolization' of design culture. At the same time, he was developing a mechanism for an office chair, the research into which so fascinated him that it opened up whole new areas of investigation. Since the demands of industry in Spain tended to call for the intervention of larger, perhaps multi-disciplinary studios, the dissolution of Grupo Berenguer may seem untypical. However, Pensi and Liévore continued to work in the same attic studios in the centre of Barcelona on their research-led projects, developing the communicative elements of design which preoccupied both of them in different ways.

The incorporation of the communicative element of design to create emblematic pieces is sometimes less subtle than in the Toledo, the Gaulino, the Trampolín chairs or the Zeleste lamp. Eduardo Samsó's Bregado sofa for Tagono, of 1987, with its brown and astrakhan hump, made a specific reference to bull fighting, suggesting something 'typically Spanish'. A self-confessed fan of bullfighting, Samsó was concerned to create something that was instantly recognizable as Spanish. If there was an element of irony in this attitude, then it was also to be found in the work of the French designer Marie-Christine Dorner for the Tarragona-based company, Scarabat. Younger designers, as absorbers of images, at times parody a stereotyped view of Spain's cultural identity.

While designers born in the 1940s, such as Tusquets, Josep Lluscà or Tresserra, tended to create plays on established visual languages of design (mixing, say, elements of Modernista styles with Rationalist typologies), some Spanish designers born in the 1950s and 60s looked wider. Perhaps this is because they underwent their formal training during the transition period in Spain, in which they were absorbers of many new images during a period of profound social change: in film, television, magazines and so on. Young Spaniards in the 1980s also travelled more than ever before – the travel agents' advertisements invariably exorted: 'If you are young, travel!'. A store of new styles and sounds was being brought back.

At the same time, different generations possessed different views of history. Those who had spent their active working life through the *años de desarollo*, economic crisis and the transition, had a clear linear sense of their own development through them. Younger designers came into the post-transitional Spain of the later 1980s sideways, without the experience of that history. Although knowing that history, they had a more fragmented view of it. Part of the appeal of Pedro Almodovar's 1986 film, *Mujeres alborde de un ataque de nervios*, was its bricolage-like view of history, placing 1960s typography and dress alongside Spanish design icons of the 1980s, all filmed in a cinematographic style akin to that of the 1950s Realists. Likewise, the artefacts of yesterday which were still available – religious medals, door-knockers, pictures of has-been *toreros* – become re-contextualized. They did not necessarily lose their associative value, but the re-use of such images suggests an ironic play on their original meaning. The notion of 'typical Spanish' in a Spain of autonomous regions, recuperation of regional languages and de-centralization was, for many young Spanish, both anachronistic and amusing. Eduardo Samsó's Bregado sofa plays on this concept. In the same vein, Pedro Miralles (b.1955), who worked from Madrid and Valencia, designed furniture with literary, popular music or cinematic references. A series of three interlocking tables he designed for Punt Mobles in 1988 was called the Andrews Sisters, their forms to some extract reflecting the singing group's era, though they were also seen as a play on all concepts of three, from the Holy Trinity to the *ménage-à-trois*.

That younger designers produced projects that expressed vigour and restlessness is certain: Sergi Devesa's furniture and lighting for Disform and Metalarte or Antoni Flores's lamps for Gargot (which specialized in producing work by younger designers) demonstrated this. Younger designers are more willing to work longer hours for less money than established names: this is attractive for some companies for obvious reasons, but – more positively – such designers also symbolize a freshness of approach for them. Moreover, it is significant that the producer was prepared to risk commissioning daring work from younger designers, as had manufacturers in Italy, France and Britain in the 1950s.

The sense of 'youth' and energy was, however, not exclusive to younger designers. In the case of Pedro Miralles's Andrews Sisters, the tables formed part of the steady strategic development of Punt Mobles. Through the 1970s its founders, Vicent Martínez and Lola Castello, produced their own designs from a small workshop in Valencia. The basic intention of Punt Mobles was to manufacture modern kit furniture in series. In Valencia this was to be an even more radical move than the example of Disform in Barcelona. Despite being the centre of Spain's furniture industry, Valencia was not renowned for its adventurousness (it had the dubious reputation of having furnished much of Hollywood). But it was the home of Spain's major international furniture fair, which followed Milan at the end of September and had its own Fernando Amat-like design guru, Luis Adelantado, who exhibited and sold various collections as well as taking other initiatives in design. In 1986, with Vicent Martínez's Halley table, a pack-down circular table resembling a cross between a satellite and a Leonardo invention, Punt Mobles launched a more consciously designerly line. Henceforth, the sophistication and prices of their objects rose steadily. As with others, in 1986 after many years of steady development, Vicent Martínez received the green light to move further upmarket with more vigorous designs. Having secured a position in the European market, he could launch more daring projects. The Halley table was an emblematic statement of that move.

Mobles 114 produced objects which later gained an emblematic quality, but stayed within the trajectory of the enterprise. Its founders were Josep Mª Massana and Josep Mª Tremoleda, both ex-students of the first course in industrial design run at the Massana School, 1965-69. After four years working as an industrial design team, they established '114', a furniture shop and interior design studio. Their aims were to edit and sell furniture and lighting through the shop, very much like Carlos Riart's approach of concentrating on the quality of design rather than the highest commercial potential of the product. At the same time, however, it was important that a market for their products already existed. When Massana and Tremoleda, with Mariano Ferrer, designed the Gira lamp in 1977 it was within the Mobles 114 line of objects that were simple, easily understood and of unsophisticated technology. In Massana and Tremoleda's Gira lamp, they were interested in providing an alternative to the ubiquitous Flexo lamp. The latter had been manufactured by various companies throughout Spain and was a design that had evolved since before the Civil War; its simplicity and highly economic price made it a standard feature of students' desks and offices of the *Guardia Civil*. While the Gira could never rival the Flexo in price, the juxtaposition of the square base and conical shade and the possibility of inclining the stem at increasingly precarious angles made this a longstanding Spanish favourite. Returning to Almodovar's film *Mujeres al borde...*, we find the Gira a protagonist, reflecting the tension with its menacing lean. By 1989, Mobles 114 was taking up a case of plagiarism: that a Spanish furniture manufacturer should accuse a foreign company of plagiarism was certainly a reversal of the norm.

Other pieces by Mobles 114 demonstrated both vigour and rigour: vigour in their lyrical idiosyncrasies and rigour in their insistent simplicity. This style at

Flexo lamp
Various producers
Date unknown
Having evolved from various precedents, this highly economical lamp became a standard feature of the Spanish visual landscape from the 1940s. In the 1980s it was produced in colours that included white, red and pink.

Fina chair
Metal, with upholstered seat
Gemma Bernal and Ramón Isern
Grupo T
1988
Founded in 1979, Grupo T specialized in metal pieces that were of simple construction and easily understood, such as those designed by Bernal/Isern.

least may tend towards a Mediterranean Rationalism that may be detected elsewhere.

The tendency towards Mediterranean Rationalism could be found in work ranging from Miguel Milà, through J. García Garay, to Bernal-Isern and to Josep Lluscà at times. This was the result of different influences. Miguel Milà was an inheritor of the modified Rationalism of Josep Antoni Coderch, stretching back to the 1950s.

In other cases, this so-called Mediterranean Rationalism may simply have been conditioned by the materials available in Barcelona. Since it had an important metal transformation industry and many accompanying small metalworking workshops, Barcelonese manufacturers were prone to take advantage of the infrastructure. Conversely, the lack of high-grade woodworking facilities or synthetic materials, as compared in particular with northern Italy, prevented development in this direction. Thus from 1979, J. García Garay edited his designs using a network of metalworking workshops. Once he had built a working relationship with them, his interest in Rationalist typologies would develop within the parameters set by the workshops. Thus his lamps became metallic essays which demonstrated complex functional demands, such as multi-directional lighting capacities or mixing ambiental and directional lighting. Gemma Bernal and Ramón Isern consistently claimed utmost neutrality as designers, allowing the relationship of the product required and the material to intervene. The end result of such a working method was sometimes, but not always, a minimal, Rationalistic form.

Josep Lluscà's Andrea chair, designed in 1986 and produced from 1988 by Andreu World, was an exploration of an unpublished three-legged Side chair of 1944 by Charles Eames. Lluscà departed from Eames's more Rationalistic project by giving it stability and sensuality. The problem of giving stability to a three-legged chair has preoccupied many designers. Philippe Starck and many others had managed this by raising the back leg high behind the backrest. Lluscà moved from this solution by taking the back leg to the critical height and taking a strong curve from the backrest through the arms. With motifs such as the support for the backrest and the organic treatment of the seat and backrest, the Andrea recalls expressive features in Modernista design. Thus, by 'banging' together different visual languages and modifying them, Lluscà suggests a Mediterranean Rationalism, and yet steps beyond it.

A member of the first generation of Eina students of 1968, Lluscà highly valued his experience there. 'Even though from a technical point of view the teaching at Eina could have been better, from a cultural or conceptual point of view it was – phew – flash! something incredible! .. and we could learn the technical side as we went along later', he enthused. The eye-opening experience he had at Eina encouraged his conceptual and practical dexterity. His work in the early 1970s took him into just about every design specialism possible. This was as much the result of the need to diversify in order to keep working, as his own catholic interests. By the 1980s, he was more or less able to choose commissions and what he might do with them. While he produced many important projects in packaging and product design, towards the end of the decade he found himself specializing mostly in furniture.

He continued to show signs of a cross-over of skills in the three or four investigations he would keep on the boil. A year after the Andrea chair, he used the same strong curve in the backrest in the equally successful BCN chair for Enea.

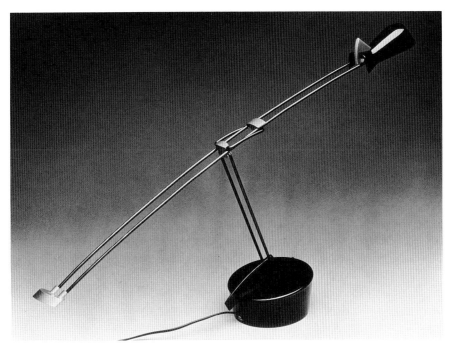

Ketupa lamp
Halogen bulb, moveable arm and shade
Josep Lluscà and Joaquín Berao
Metalarte S.A.
1989

Moving away from the drawing board and towards three-dimensional modelling – aided by an experience of designing a table lamp with the silversmith, Joaquín Berao – Lluscà pursued more curvilinear forms. This was to some extent facilitated by producers using computer-aided production, as in the case of the Andrea chair. At the same time, if production runs on furniture grew, Lluscà nevertheless maintained an individualistic, even artisanal approach to his projects, treating each detail with precision while keeping an open book on the conceptual influences on the object.

Josep Lluscà is only one example of the difficulty in defining Spanish furniture designers by type. Spain is unlike Milan, where there were such studios as Sottsass Associati, Michele de Lucchi or even Olivetti to act as umbrellas in bringing designers to work together, to have group shows and to produce manifestos. Professional organizations, such as ADIFAD or ADP, and schools such as Eina, existed as platforms for debate and self-promotion, but there have never been any manifestos of group intent. While the majority of Spain's more avant-garde furniture designers were concentrated in Barcelona, they worked from small studios scattered across the city. Many, including Lluscà, concentrated on furniture design, yet resisted any temptation to form larger studios.

If anything, furniture designers were bound by historical experience. The majority of the most celebrated designers – like most of Spain's government ministers during the 1980s – were born in 1940s of (as we have already noted) middle-class, progressive families. They received architectural training or design education in the 1960s and developed multi-disciplinary work in the 1970s, working through the economic depression of that decade with the impetus provided by the cultural euphoria of the transition. Many had been closely involved with the development of production companies which were to provide the basis for the international publication of their work. They emerged in the 1980s with at least fifteen years unbridled conceptual experience. Italy would provide the blueprint for the technical standards to be attained. It would also provide much of the theoretical debate. The play on visual language, a game learnt by the coincidence of a frustration with but not wholesale rejection of Modernist principles and the arrival of new semiological and structuralist approaches to design, was never dropped.

The choice of visual languages to quote was an open one. With perhaps the exception of Studio Per, Spanish designers did not preoccupy themselves so much with Pop imagery or anti-design as their Italian relatives. Designing was intrinsically radical during the years of late-Francoism, but well-made, visually interesting chairs had to be produced before they could be subverted. Nor did Spanish furniture express any Italianate classicism or machine imagery.

In Barcelona, two strong design legacies were available. One was the Modernism of Sert and GATCPAC: symbolically charged with its oppositional nature. The other was Modernisme, which pervaded the cityscape from complete blocks to the detailing of door handles. Modernisme had the added political charge of being a specifically Catalan expression. It also implied an attention to detail and an accompanying artisanal tradition. In designing and producing furniture, both legacies were recuperated, either from a formal point of view, often ending up in the quotation or exploration of their visual imagery, or in terms of their symbolic or ideological identities. At the same time, emergent younger designers were exposed to and incorporated new visual imagery made available by Spain's cultural opening out in the 1980s.

Whilst there might have been a methodological unity amongst designers, strategies adopted by manufacturers, both in the commercialization and in the production of furniture, were more diverse.

In 1989 Josep Lluscà brought out the Lola office chair with a flourish. It was launched in the Mies pavilion in Barcelona, with accompanying music and a lavish publication featuring photographs of friends and mentors including Oriol Bohigas, Frederico Correa and Albert Ràfols Casamada in dialogue with the chair. The Lola was produced by Oken, a new editing company descended from Norma Europ, for whom Lluscà designed in the 1970s. The catalogue to the Lola explained about Oken: 'as an editor, its strategy is better explained by basing it more on a model of conduct rather than on a model of production …it is a multi-directional formula of absolute operative liberty, created in order to pursue good design'. In other words, editing could break down the technical parameters of specialization, thus liberating the designer or producer to pursue the 'higher' interests of form.

The creation of new producing companies, based on editing rather than centralized production, certainly shows that it was by no means an antiquated strategy in the 1980s. Indeed, some companies such as Metalarte, whose production had traditionally been centralized, moved more in the direction of editing during this decade. At the same time, greater technical and aesthetic demands were made on artisanal or semi-artisanal workshops by design-led furniture editing companies. This in turn led to the workshops attaining much higher standards in the finished product. On the other hand, the momentum for these higher standards constantly came from the designers and editors themselves. It was a constant battle to ensure that, at the end of the day, the product could compete on international markets, with the Germans, the French and, not least, the Italians. Since the momentum for improvement did not come from the workshops themselves, it was unlikely that they would move beyond production for furniture and other luxury goods to more sophisticated products, such as tooling and machinery.

Producing furniture to acceptable international standards was also a problem encountered by centralized manufacturers. One of the major attractions of Spanish furniture for international buyers in the later 1980s was its relative cheapness as compared with Italian pieces in particular. The biggest complaint, though, was that it often did not compete in terms of safety and durability with Italian work. Crude jointing, poor welding and badly finished upholstery in some cases detracted from the initial pleasure of vigorous, interesting forms. At the furniture fairs in the 1980s, international buyers and distributors were eager to sign up *their* Spanish discovery, later finishing the relationship in a huff as they discovered that it didn't hold water.

Companies such as Disform, Casas/Mobilplast and Mobles 114 had demonstrated through the years that a rigorous design-led policy could compete in international markets. With these historical precedents, existing companies such as Enea and Andreu World were encouraged to incorporate a design-led policy into their industrial reconversion. When Spain's design boom flowered from 1986, companies such as Amat, Punt Mobles and Tagono produced increasingly provocative and emblematic pieces to prove their designerly worth. Some companies ran the risk of producing rather frivolous, fashionable pieces in order to do this. Akaba was unapologetic about its strong projects, intending to keep one step ahead of this risk: Santa & Cole edited provocative pieces in their own right whilst keeping a check on the reflective components of design.

The eclecticism of new Spanish furniture was firstly the result of the inputs of individual designers (rather than design groups), who shared common experiences and ways of seeing but applied them in their own distinct ways. Secondly, producers, often bound closely to designers, quickly responded with flexibility to the changing status of design in Spain in equally diverse directions. In either case, results were varying in quality, but generally demonstrating that there was life beyond Postmodernism. Having made a solid impact at the furniture fairs, towards the end of the 1980s Spanish design needed to prove its strengths in other disciplines in order to consolidate its position in the 1990s.

Left: Opaco screen
Beech, lacquered and varnished
Carlos Riart
Muebles Casas S.A.
Designed 1976
Forming part of Riart's important 1976 exhibition,
Primera Colección de Muebles Especiales', this
screen is still in production.

Above: Colilla lamp
Glass tube with neon bulbs
Carlos Riart
Santa & Cole S.A.
Designed 1976
For two years Riart produced this lamp at home and
sold it by mail order. In 1979 Gabriel Ordeig
introduced several improvements with a view to
meeting a growing demand, fostered by word of
mouth.

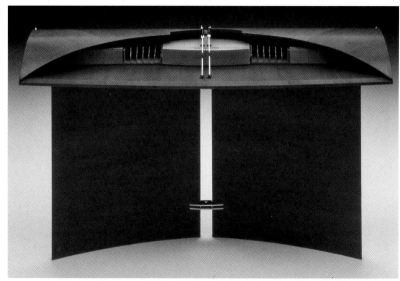

Left and below: Butterfly Carlton-house
Walnut, sycamore interior with nickel-plated
details and leather finish
Jaime Tresserra
J. Tresserra S.L.
1988

Like Riart, Tresserra looked to a recuperation
of traditional wood-working skills in
producing his made-to-order pieces. Each
project, however, became progressively more
technically complex and visually provocative.

Top and above: Elliptic cabinet
Walnut, with silver and leather
edgings
Jaime Tresserra
J. Tresserra S.L.
1988

Above: Jon Ild shelving
Lacquered epoxy iron upright, shelves in lacquered DM
Philippe Starck
Disform S.A.
1983

Left: Chincheta table
Single sheet of aluminium, with epoxy finish
Sergi Devesa
Disform S.A.
1989

Disform was a pioneer in editing during the 1970s, drawing on networks of indigenous artisanal workshops. It was also important in promoting the work of young Spanish designers, such as Sergi Devesa, as well as foreign designers in Spain, such as Philippe Starck.

Left: Varius chair
Expanded polyurethane interior, metal frame, with leather armrest covers
Oscar Tusquets
Casas S.A.
1983

Below: Vortice table
Oak, with elm root, oak or Spanish walnut inlay
Oscar Tusquets
Carlos Jané S.A.
1989

Right: Gaulino stools
Oak, with calf hide upholstering and brass footrest
Oscar Tusquets
Carlos Jané S.A.
1989

Tusquets's eclecticism has led him to be labelled as Spain's representative of Postmodernism.

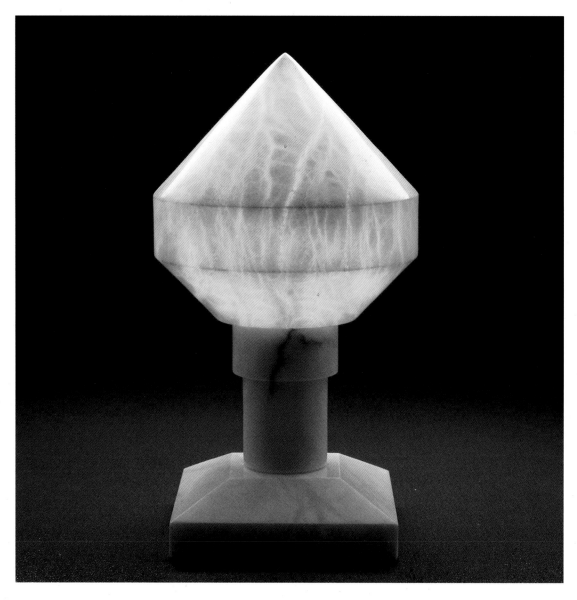

Above: Zeleste lamp
Alabaster
Angel Jové and Santiago Roqueta
Santa & Cole S.A.
Designed 1968
Originally designed for the avant-garde bar,
Zeleste, with the spiritual influence of Ettore
Sottsass, this lamp subsequently became a cult
object.

Opposite left: La bella durmiente (sleeping beauty)
lamp
PVC, with interior strip light
Lamp designed by Gabriel Ordeig with painting by
Viçenc Viaplana
Santa & Cole S.A.
Designed 1985
This lamp forms part of a series of eight decorated
by different designers and artists.

Opposite, right: Egipcia lamp
Incandescent bulb
Pedro Miralles
Santa & Cole S.A.
1987
Inspired by studies of ancient Egyptian art, this
lamp is intended to sit close to a wall.

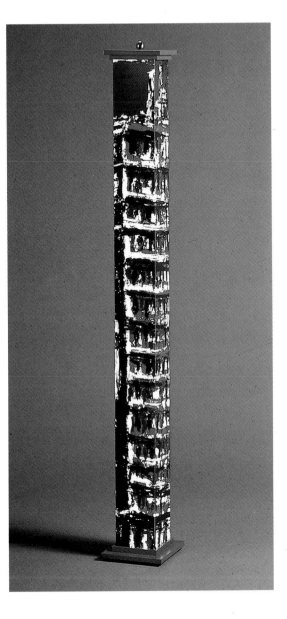

Left: Trampolín chair
Bleached ash, with painted steel base
Pepe Cortés and Javier Mariscal
Akaba S.A.
1986

Right, top: Frenesi stool
Chrome steel base, with leather seat
Transatlántic
Akaba S.A.
1986

Right, bottom: M.O.R. sofa
Steel frame, fabric seat, leather back
Pepe Cortés and Javier Mariscal
Akaba S.A.
1986

Sometimes accused of producing frivolous pieces, Akaba of San Sebastián none the less edits furniture that is uncompromisingly experimental in formal conception.

Left: Toledo chair
Cast aluminium
Jorge Pensi
Amat S.A.
1988
The Toledo broke new ground in outdoor furniture,
bringing the late-1980s European interest in curves
to cast aluminium.

Above: Helsinoor armchair
Soft leather upholstery
Alberto Liévore and Jorge Pensi
Perobell S.C.
1987
Pensi and Liévore were instrumental in the
transformation of Perobell from middle-of-the-road
home-furnishings company in the 1970s to design-
led manufacturer in the 1980s.

Right: Orfila chair
Cast aluminium, with wooden seat, back and arms
Jorge Pensi
Thonet
1989
Pensi continued his investigations in cast
aluminium for the German company Thonet.

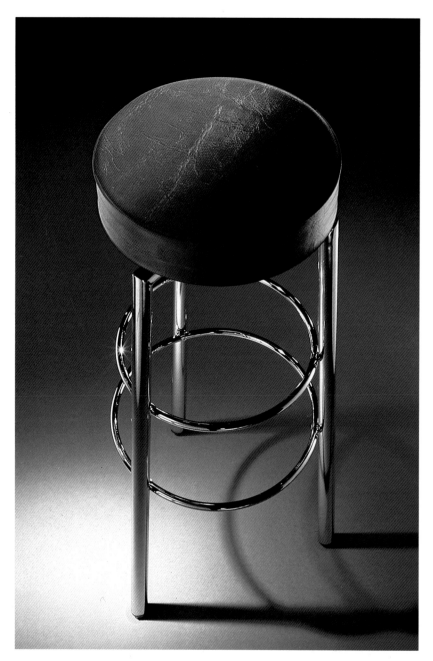

Left: Corbu stool
Tubular steel base
Alberto Liévore
Indartu S.A.
1989

Above: Manthis table
Chromed steel
Alberto Liévore
Perobell S.C.
1988
Adjustable to various heights, this is a development from a field-table.

Right: Manolete chair
Alberto Liévore
Perobell S.C.
1988
The Manolete's lack of depth is explained by the fact that it is conceived as a temporary seat for spaces such as hallways and bedrooms, thereby recuperating a lost typology of furniture.

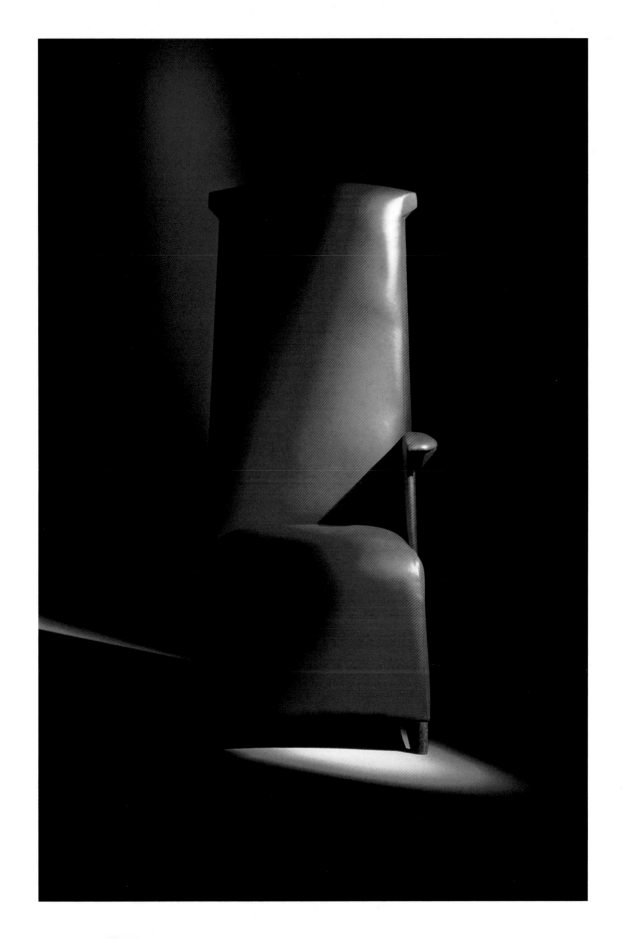

Bregado sofa
Suede, with astrakhan hump
Eduardo Samsó
Tagono S.A.
1988
Another unapologetic statement of 'typical Spanish'
by Samsó.

Left: Andrews Sisters tables
Bubinga wood
Pedro Miralles
Punt Mobles S.A.
1988
Pedro Miralles moves within the art, film and literary circles that are found typically in Madrid. His designs, therefore, often have overtones to match. In this case, it is not just the singing Andrews Sisters, but all well-known groups of three, from the Holy Trinity to the ménage-à-trois.

Right: Halley table
Glass or veneer ashwood top, ashwood frame with metal legs
Vicent Martínez
Punt Mobles S.A.
1986
This table signalled a move towards more sophisticated pieces as Punt Mobles consolidated its international standing.

Left: Gira lamp
Aluminium shade, chrome steel stem
Josep Mª Massana, Josep Mª Tremoleda,
Mariano Ferrer
Mobles 114
1979
The technically simple, yet formally provocative Gira
lamp has become a timeless classic.

Left: Gina lamps
Moulded aluminium
Antoni Flores
Gargot S.A.
1987
The Gina's telescopic extensions allow the lamp to
become either a reading light or an ambiental light.

Above right: Havana bench
Laminated woods
Josep Mª Massana and Josep Mª Tremoleda
Mobles 114
1979

Left: Nit (night) table
Wood, with metal base
Ash, with aluminium base
Gabriel Ordeig
Mobles 114
1988

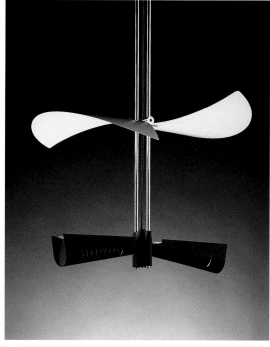

Left: Gala chair
Gemma Bernal and Ramón Isern
Sellex S.A.
1988
The designers' preference for simple solutions
governed by the materials often results in pieces
which in turn suggest, at times, an aesthetic of
1950s Rationalism.

Above: Enterprise hanging lamp
Chromed metal
Reflectors swing through 360 degrees
J. García Garay
García Garay S.A.
1988

Right: Fenix hanging lamp
Chromed metal
J. García Garay
García Garay S.A.
1987
J. García Garay's interest in Rationalist typologies is
bought to lyrical essays in metal.

Right: Andrea chair
Chrome steel legs, beech seat and back
Josep Lluscà
Andreu World S.A.
Designed 1986
The Andrea supremely demonstrates a common approach of Spanish designers of his generation: that of mixing historical styles, which sometimes may seem conflicting. In this case, Lluscà re-examines a Charles Eames three-legged side chair of the 1940s, and in combining Gaudíesque elements in the seat, back and support, gives the seat stability and a sensuous effect. With the aid of computer-controlled machining, the use of curved wood also reflects some present-day currents.

Above left: BCN chair
Chrome steel frame, with leather upholstery
Josep Lluscà
Enea S.C.
1988

Above right: Lola office chair
Aluminium foot and arms, polyurethane foam seat and back
Josep Lluscà
Oken S.A.
1989

Right: Lola system of office chairs
Josep Lluscà
Oken S.A.
1989

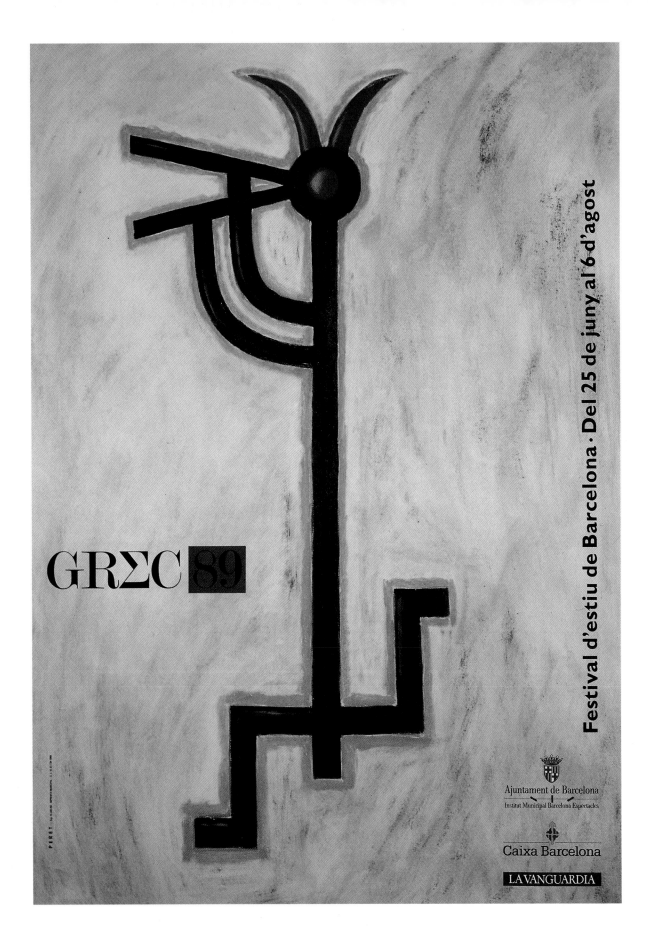

GRΣC 89

Festival d'estiu de Barcelona · Del 25 de juny al 6 d'agost

Ajuntament de Barcelona
Institut Municipal Barcelona Espectacles

Caixa Barcelona

LA VANGUARDIA

graphics

Image and Identities

gRAPHIC DESIGN ENCOMPASSES A WIDE range of expressions. As a form of visual communication it may include work as varied as corporate identity programmes for large companies, book jackets and posters for night-clubs. Until the 1990s, graphic designers in Spain were characterized by their lack of specialization. Even by the late 1980s there were very few studios with over 20 professionals that were likely to concentrate on larger, corporate identity projects. To some extent this activity was already monopolized by multinational publicity agencies such as J. Walter Thompson, Landor Associates and Saatchi & Saatchi Compton. Instead, graphic designers tended to work individually, or in studios of two or three. If there were some signs of larger studios, it was partly in response to the growing international pressure exerted by foreign companies, partly in response to the growing opportunities for big projects. At the same time, there remained a tendency for graphic designers to distance themselves from indigenous publicity agencies – where many of them had trained – to set up their own individual studios.

The monopoly held by multinational agencies on the most important accounts meant that the arenas for originality in expression for indigenous designers under the *dictatura* were in underground magazines and comics, the more progressive publishing houses and smaller commercial ventures. In other words, Spanish graphic designers flourished on their own ground, rather than in the open territory of mass consumption. Apart from emanating from smaller, individualistic studios, therefore, their work was often characterized by a certain oppositional flavour and restless energy.

The propagandist poster was an important ideological tool for the Republicans during the Spanish Civil War (1936-39). Associated mostly with El Sindicato de Dibujantes Profesionales (the Union of Professional Draughtsman), designers such as Josep Renau and Arturo Ballester produced posters of varying technical quality. Aesthetically, though, they provided colourful and vigorous

Left: Poster for Grec '89 cultural festival in Barcelona
Peret
Ajuntament de Barcelona
1989

images, sometimes informed by Soviet propagandist posters. With the Francoist defeat of the Republican forces, this movement was pushed underground, its protagonist in the field of photomontage, Josep Renau, going into exile in Mexico.

In the context of Spain in the 1940s and 50s, culturally isolated and economically stagnant, it is not surprising that the first steps towards a distinctive indigenous graphic design movement were taken at a submerged, oppositional level. Ricard Giralt Miracle, son of Francesc Giralt III, a prestigious lithographer, began in the early 1950s to produce designs using typographic collage, juxtapositions of images and bold colours. While many of these designs remained unpublished, they formed the basis for activity of a young graphic design avant-garde in Barcelona, which included Alexandre Cirici and his Studio Zen. The collage and photomontage work instigated by Giralt Miracle was carried through to the first Catalan publications tolerated under Franco, which emerged in the 1960s. These included the books of the publishers Edicions 62, designed by Jordi Fornas, and the magazine *Serra d'Or*.

Meanwhile, in Madrid Daniel Gil produced covers for the books of Alianza Editorial and Alberto Corazón designed for various publishing ventures, including his own. They exhibited a more controlled use of image than the vigorous collage work to be found in Barcelona. Their use of powerful photographic illustrations in their book jackets played on the use of image as sign, allowing a reading of the cover before the text. Brought to Barcelona in particular by Enric Satué, this acted to stabilize the (at times) over-enthusiastic vigour sometimes proposed in alternative publications there.

Having studied at the Belles Arts faculty of Barcelona University and worked in a publicity agency, Enric Satué was invited in 1970 to design a new architecture and design magazine, *CAU*. It was established as the official journal of the Colegio de Aparejadores de Barcelona, which had just held the first elections for its governing body, unanimously won by progressive candidates. This meant that *CAU* was to be a radical mouthpiece, each edition addressing itself beyond architecture and design to issues in society, and, more specifically, Francoist society. As such, *CAU* employed a language and imagery of play, irony and, above all, innovation, like the Escuela de Barcelona at the same time. Accordingly, Satué approached each edition entirely differently, creating a new format for each one, though with a marked tendency towards photomontage deriving, in particular, from Milton Glaser.

Enric Satué went on to design the journal *Arquitectura Bis* from 1974 to 1985. Here the layout demonstrated a mixture of sobriety (in its architectonic proportions) with restlessness (in the constant moving of the header). When he came to design the new *Diari de Barcelona*, a daily newspaper in Catalan, in

1492·1992

Logo for the fifth centenary of the discovery of America
José Mª Cruz Novillo
1986
Alongside Alberto Corazón and Daniel Gil, José Mª Cruz Novillo has been instrumental in promoting and maintaining activities in graphic design in Madrid since the 1960s.

Poster announcing the *Dia del Libro* (day of the book)
Ricard Giralt Miracle
1964
Using collage, photomontage, or — in this case — a vigorous painterly format, Giralt Miracle was a torchbearer of Barcelona's more gestural graphic style from the 1950s.

Far left: Teatro María Guerrero
Poster
Alberto Corazón
1978
This poster incorporates Republican Civil War posters, as well as Picasso and Goya.

Left: *Defiende tu Colegio*
(defend your primary school)
Poster
Alberto Corazón
1978
Corazón's portfolio is extensive, ranging from his own publishing house to extensive corporate identity programmes via his company, Investigación Gráfica S.A. At the same time, however, he also produced cultural and political posters.

Above: *Arquitecturas Bis*
Barcelona-based architectural
journal
Enric Satué
1974-75
Satué designed this journal until
1985. The layout was deliberately
architectonic in its proportions.

Far right: *El Temps*
Valencia-based weekly magazine
Enric Satué
1989
With a strong awareness of the
commercial 1980s and the
repertoire of logos and trademarks
thus stored in the collective
psyche, Satué used suggestion
skilfully in his series of covers for *El Temps*.

1987, he changed its shield every day – each one was designed by a different artist or designer, amongst them Antoni Tàpies, Miguel Barceló and Mariscal. It is through such projects that he brought about fresh, innovatory approaches to Spanish graphic design. The use of strong, yet controlled imagery interplaying with text was picked up in the 1980s in the work of Josep Mª Mir and Joaquim Nolla, in particular in their work for the architectural magazine, *Cuaderns d'Arquitectura*.

Thus the historical roots of avant-garde graphic design in Spain lay mostly in oppositional, small-scale activities. This continued into the 1980s: the 'oppositional' character of creativity was no longer so potent, but the creation of new images and graphic expressions still came mostly from a fragmented and eclectic array of individuals, studios and some larger consultancies.

The dispersion of graphic designers into small studios partly reflects their own preference for working individually. It also reflects the scale and fragmentation of industry and commerce. Relatively cheap rents for flats in most of Spain's cities also encouraged small studios, whereas larger studios in more modern office-style buildings were prohibitively expensive for young designers. The arrival of the fax maintained the dispersion, since it allowed easier communication between separated units. Within this context, it is hardly surprising that there was a propensity for non-specialist graphic designers. They would work as easily on a magazine as a logo for a bar. Such diversity encouraged a freshness of approach.

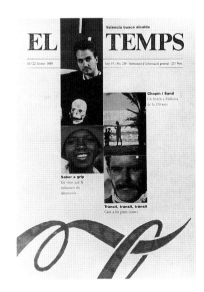

A smaller studio is unlikely to invest in technology such as Computer Aided Design. In fact, among many designers, young and old alike, there was almost a universal disdain for such gadgetry, fuelled, for instance, by its unconvincing use in the animated sequences provided by the national television network. In any case, they simply couldn't afford it. A more freehand, painterly approach, with the inclusion of collage and photomontage, was therefore often favoured. The painterly approach was to be found widely, from the posters and illustrations of Peret and Mariscal in Barcelona, through to the packaging of Marisa Gallén and Sandra Figuerola in Valencia. Collage and photomontage work was again undertaken by Peret, as well as by Guillem Vidal, Ricard Badia, Josep Bagà, Cecília Sales and many others.

Having trained in the important studio of Josep Pla Narbona in the 1960s, Peret moved to post-May 1968 Paris. After seven years working in a range of different studios and also as a freelance, he returned to Barcelona. Although his graphic style changed radically almost from commission to commission, two unifying factors are his investigation into painting and preference for it as a source, and his method of constructing the image as if it were a painting. Thus he would work with oil on canvas, or with coloured paper and scissors, as if the design was to be an original work of art rather than a mechanically reproduced graphic image. This preference made each image emblematic. The large numbers of commissions he received from the Barcelona City Council and his work as an illustrator for the newspaper *La Vanguardia*, made him known as a producer and provoker of new images and emblems for the city. At times these images were met with disapproval. They included one featuring a middle-age man with erection in the arms of a young girl, which the editor of *La Vanguardia* refused to publish, and another that was a spoof on Velázquez's *Surrender of Breda* for an issue of the same newspaper on Spain in the European Community. In the latter case, the disapproval came from Dalí. Other images received wholesale acclaim. For Barcelona's 1985 show of art and design by young Mediterraneans, La Biennal, he produced a representation of Zeus's abduction of Europa. The poster's blue background revived the sense of the Mediterranean as a geographical environment and the scene of a dense, ancient and renewed tradition, from which the constructivist Zeus as bull had abducted Europa. It thus signified a refocusing of European cultural activity to the Mediterranean.

While acknowledging new movements afoot in Spain, Peret was hostile to any opportunism afforded by them. For his part, rather than use his success to expand his studio in numbers, he took over a derelict shoe-factory in the heart of Barcelona in 1989, and renovated it to become a seat of artistic investigation more akin to the studios of the Renaissance painters than Warhol's factory. Thus Peret's provocative avant-gardism was assured.

Posters for the Gran Teatre del
Liceu, Barcelona
América Sánchez
1984
As well as being a talented
photographer, Sánchez also has a
fascination for 'demotic' graphic
design, such as the typographic
irregularity of woodblock printed
posters for rural boxing matches.
At times, the influence may be
seen in his own typographic work.

Small studios were also unlikely to invest in complex marketing techniques. To compensate, therefore, the designer relied on the strength of the image. At the same time, this approach corresponded to the requirements of wholesale image-changing undertaken at all levels of Spanish industry, commerce and institutions during the 1980s. (As already noted in Chapter 1, officials of all Spain's design centres, from Barcelona to Valencia to Bilbao, believed that industry and commerce in the *reconversión industrial* run up to 1992 were more prone to change their image before their identity; they would hire graphic designers to change their company logos before getting to the guts of their products.) Complete overhauls of most companies, despite incentives offered by design centres, were unlikely. Graphics, then, soon became the largest sector in the design business. Furthermore, small studios suited the dominance of small and middle-size businesses over large – in 1978, 94 per cent of businesses in Spain employed less than 50, with only 2 per cent employing more than 500.

Many immigrants to Spain arriving in the 1960s and 1970s brought new strengths to graphic design. These included Yves Zimmermann, who through his teaching at Elisava and Eina brought the rigorous and disciplined use of typography as a formal element from Switzerland. The German, Reinhardt Gäde, and the South Americans, Mario Ezkenazi, Carlos Rolando and Ricardo Rousselet, all had solid experience behind them and pushed standards on. Of particular importance in the pioneering of corporate image design was the Argentinian-born América Sánchez. His prolific work for small- and medium-size companies demonstrated to individualistic designers the viability of working in this area.

The expansion of opportunities in industry for graphic designers was prefigured partly by design work coming from new fashion shops and bars in the early 1980s. One designer who gained particular recognition in these fields was Pati Nuñez. She provided logos and shopping bags for many of Barcelona's design 'ports of call', including the club Otto Zutz, the café Network, as well as fashion shops Moscow and Stone House. At times much of the typography employed came close to that of the English cult figure, Neville Brody. Amongst Barcelona's younger designers *The Graphic Language of Neville Brody* (1988) was a well-thumbed publication; in the florid townscape of Barcelona, Brodyesque typography provided a stark, urban point of reference when used to promote new bars and fashion outlets.

Logo for Barcelona's Olympic
candidature
América Sánchez
1984

graphics

1 9 2 9

NETWORK
CAFE
1 9 4 2

network®
1 9 6 1

NETWORK
1 9 7 2

NETWORK
CAFE
1 9 8 6

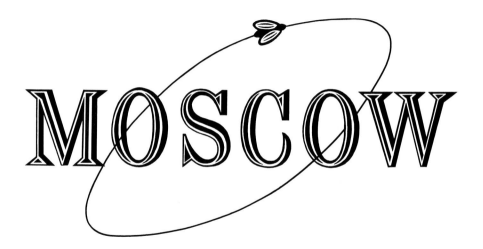

Nuñez was an enthusiastic traveller and collector of books, comics and magazines. Her frequent travels and ability to absorb many different images were translated into her design work, as the same characteristics were with many younger designers. Thus her designs often became plays on images, words and ideas. Her logo for Moscow played on the Spanish word 'mosca', meaning fly. In collaboration with Alfons Sostres and the interior designers Alfredo Arribas and Eduard Samsó, she created a fictitious story for the new café Network, in which the history of its development was written and reflected in the development of its logos through the decades.

Graphic designers in the 1980s also achieved greater name-recognition in Spain through the public commissions of governmental, council and other institutional bodies. In order to expound the virtues of good design, as part of Spain's wholesale reconversion, official institutions had to be seen to be its most enthusiastic consumers. In some cases governing bodies in competition would attempt to 'out-design' each other, as in the case of the socialist Barcelona City Council and the centre-right Catalan Regional Government, otherwise known as the Generalitat. There was also a tendency for the Ajuntament (city council) to employ younger or more individualist designers such as Pati Nuñez or Peret, in order, partly, to present a more youthful image for posters publicizing cultural events.

Large commissions, such as replacing the sign system of Barcelona's Metro system, were commissioned by competition. In this case it was won in 1981 by the graphic designers, Josep Mª Trias and Joaquim Trias, with the fittings designed by Joan Antoni Blanc. For this work, the semiologist Miguel de Moragas undertook a preliminary study of Metro systems in other countries. The employment of a university professor to add weight to such an enterprise in Spain is not unusual. To some extent, from the academic's point of view, it is a function of the prevalence in Spain of *pluri-empleo*, where someone is apt to hold down more than one job at the same time; from the designer's point of view

Trademark for Barcelona fashion shop, Moscow
Pati Nuñez
1988

Logos for Network Café
Pati Nuñez and Alfons Sostres
1986

96

it adds intellectual status to the project. Moreover, it was a continuation of the high intellectual colour that design carried in the schools from the 1960s.

The renovation of the Metro system represented a break from the past chaos, resulting from years of neglect under Francoism. Among architects and designers, in the midst of general urban delapidation and lack of control, Spain's public transport system had always undergone heavy criticism. The re-designing of such elements was open to strong public scrutiny, and consequently graphic designers and their work became known to the public and to commerce. Design work for future projects, in particular the 1992 Barcelona Olympic Games, was to receive even greater attention.

Josep Mª Trias's winning logo for the 1992 Olympic Games gained widespread approval, partly because of his own brand of marketing, which meant more 'being in touch with the people' than complex market surveys. As a member of the multi-disciplinary studio, Quod, which was unique in Spain for the importance it gave to marketing, Trias – more than many – was aware of what marketing meant. At the same time, the logo relied equally on a measure of poetic intuition. Trained, like many significant designers, in the studio of Josep Pla Narbona, he learnt from him the value of drawing with 'one part head, one part heart'. The logo reflected this balance.

Many previous Olympic logos had imposed geometric, unreferential forms. Trias's involved a more colourful, painterly attitude, through the inclusion of a feature which was at once an abstract mark and a representation of a leaping athlete. It was neither a pictogram nor a doodle, therefore. The shapes supposed a certain 'Mediterraneanism' and in their painterliness rendered homage to Barcelona's artistic reputation: Dalí, Miró and Picasso have more to do with the city's reputation than, say, any technological or scientific tradition. The use of the Times Semi-Bold typeface evoked an antique, Roman past.

Trias derived this design from Far Eastern calligraphy, but the use of broad strokes of primary colours was immediately interpreted as falling within a Miróesque tradition. That the Catalan painter Joan Miró should have exerted an influence on Spanish and, in particular, Catalan graphic design was unavoidable. Miró himself had produced pro-Republican imagery during the Civil War and a poster for the new Catalan daily *Avui* in 1975, among other graphic works. He was well known for his anti-Francoist stance, and was one of Spain's few successful avant-garde artists to keep a strong association with the country during the *dictatura*. His artistic activities had consistently been documented and publicized, not least by Alexandre Cirici, and his artistic style was easily applicable to graphic design. While in Britain, for example, groups such as Wolff Olins and Michael Peters were turning out pallid, sketchy logos, well judged for their market, in Spain, Miró provided a more vigorous visual language. This

Sign-system for Barcelona Metro system
Josep Mª Trias, Joaquim Trias, Joan Antoni Blanc, Miguel de Moragas
1981

imagery may well have rested deep in the visual vocabulary of the Spanish, thus assuring its acceptance. Not surprisingly, it verged on becoming a dangerously overused mannerism. In particular, one finds 'Miróism' in the work of larger multinational agencies, such as Tandem's tourist logo for Spain, Landor Associates' logo for the savings bank, 'La Caixa', and, to a lesser extent, Wolff Olins's logo for Repsol.

As a prolific essayist on graphic design, Enric Satué has reflected on the meaning and significance of graphic expression in Spanish society. He holds a profound belief that the Spanish visual imagination is sensitized to the communicative potential of graphic design.

The vast level of consumption of comics that took place during Francoism and since tends to bear this out. Comics formed one of the stalwarts of the 'culture of evasion'. They were also a medium for subversion in the early 1970s, emanating, in particular, from the Rambleros – young artists/designers/illustrators who were concentrated around the Plaça Real in Barcelona and included Mariscal. These comics were derived from the underground scene of London and the United States and in the early 1980s their activities found wider publication through the adult comics *Cairo* and *Víbora*.

With a youth culture that was visually literate in this graphic style, it is not surprising that when Mariscal transferred it to posters, T-shirt prints and, eventually, an Olympic mascot, it was met with wild acclaim.

A combination of many years struggle, some good fortune and a complex public status made Mariscal Spain's most talked about creative personality. Born in Valencia, in the late 1960s he alternated his life between the hippy atmosphere of Ibiza and the Plaça Real. He put in a brief appearance as a student of graphic design at Barcelona's Massana school in the early 70s, but found specialization difficult to cope with. His creativity extended beyond graphic work to interiors, textiles, furniture and sculpture, though the unifying force in all these areas came from the sketchy, intuitive fast work of his drawing.

Since he never immersed himself in any design 'methodology', he retained a distance from current trends; rather, he nurtured eclectic interests, including Art Deco. He also saw himself as neither an artist nor a designer; he exhibited drawings, paintings and sculptures in galleries, but never called them Art; he never claimed the technical or commercial faculties of an industrial designer. His colourful, angular, sketchy graphic style, which he had been practising since the mid-1970s, his obliviousness to art/design boundaries and the unrelenting jokiness in his projects thus coincided with the Memphis adventure of 1980-83. It was from the invitation to participate with the Memphis team in 1981 that Mariscal suddenly received international recognition. For his part, until then he had never heard of Memphis and was amazed to find a group of people working in the same direction as himself. Subsequently, he became hot property, both nationally and internationally.

Mariscal's humorous comic drawings at times may seem simply to be re-worked themes, such as Mickey Mouse in his Los Garriris (though he hated Mickey Mouse). The experience demonstrated by Los Garriris was that of the drunken runaways, overwhelmed in the big city, thus drawing on Mariscal's own first encounters with Barcelona. Indeed, while he made journeys of discovery to Egypt and Mali, for instance, much of his work referred specifically to the experience of living in his adopted Catalonia. Beaches of the Costa Brava, monuments of Barcelona and frenetic traffic were common features.

There is also a historical image of Mariscal the personality, which carried considerable weight in the public imagination. His roguishness was well known. He was the designer, it seemed, who liked to go out at night for a few drinks, and who when he got bored and wanted to enjoy himself a bit, did some work. Rather than the temperamental bohemian artist, he was the erratic, but none the less artistically fecund – and humorous – renegade. As the demands of *reconversión industrial* became greater through the 1980s, design in Spain had to be presented by such institutions as the Barcelona Centre of Design more and more for its technical and commercial value rather than its cultural value. Meanwhile, the image of renegade Mariscal provided a safety valve, demonstrating that amidst the seriousness, there was still room for intuitive, ingenious creativity.

In January 1988, Mariscal's wagishness seriously backfired when he dared to pass comment on the stature of the president of Catalonia's Generalitat, Jordi Pujol, and suggested that there might be too many Catalans in Catalonia. When this reached the national press, it caused an uproar among many proud Catalans, resulting in a mass demonstration in the city centre of Barcelona calling for his apology and for his proposed 1992 Olympic mascot, Cobi, to be put into early retirement. This event represented something of a turning point in the image of him communicated by the media. Henceforth he was the childlike drawer, wide-eyed and naïve, reflecting the constant discoveries of a country 'con zapatos nuevos' (with new shoes).

At the same time, though, Mariscal's success allowed him to work on ever more ambitious projects. In the summer of 1989, his retrospective exhibition, *Cent Anys a Barcelona*, took place on a converted boat. The idea was that the project should function as a leisure amusement – it was sponsored, among

Selection of comics by Mariscal from the mid-1970s

others, by the amusement park of Tibidabo. Thus culture became leisure. Spain for two decades had sold itself to the leisure of foreign tourists on its coastal resorts. In the 1980s, it took care of its own leisure time outside football and bullfighting, feeding it with new images and identities. Joan Lerma, President of the Generalitat of Valencia, wrote in the exhibition catalogue: 'Mariscal is without doubt a significant milestone in the renovation of our most immediate reality.'

In order to take care of more ambitious projects, Mariscal established in 1989 a large studio in Barcelona's old industrial area, Poble Nou. Here he brought together creative people from many different disciplines, as well as a strong administrative back-up. He saw this as a way of freeing *himself* to concentrate on the creative end of projects; it was also a response to their growing complexity.

The bringing together of individual designers to form multi-disciplinary groups had been associated with the 1970s, as in the case, for instance, of the Grupo Abierto. To some extent it may be read as a continuance of that same euphoria in the 1980s. There was, however, a clear commercial advantage shown by the successes of various larger set-ups.

In Valencia, in 1984, two studios, Caps i Mans and Enebecé, merged, to form a multi-disciplinary collective called La Nave, steered by eleven core members. With another ten collaborators, at full strength they made up virtually 30 per cent of Valencia's designer population. Their size made them more visible than the average smaller-sized studios in Valencia, and they soon dominated commissions in the region. They were also able to attract some development help from the Valencia Regional Government.

As professional designers, La Nave's members were more or less self-taught. Aside from the Escola d'Arts i Oficis de Valencia and a few disparate private design schools, Valencia was not provisioned with schools of the historical weight of Barcelona. Young designers tended to travel to Italy with grants from the regional government or otherwise to develop their own approaches. Thus some members of La Nave, such as Sandra Figuerola and Marisa Gallén, came from a fine art background and applied this liberally to their graphic work. Organizationally and aesthetically, they did not conform to any fixed identity. They would work individually, in ready-formed partnerships or in coalitions within the collective, which meant in turn that they were able to respond to all sizes of commissions.

Valencia's reputation for having a small-town, conservative mentality is belied by its relentless nightlife and incorrigibly energetic young population. It doesn't have the new bars of Barcelona, but there is no lack of custom. 'Valencia doesn't benefit from the same cultural traditions as, say, Barcelona', Paco Bascuñán confirmed to me; 'but being outside allows a certain freshness.' And this is

Above: Logo for art gallery, Arte Xerea
Luis González (La Nave)
1989

the quality most apparent in the graphic design work of La Nave. Of particular note are Luis González's anarchically funny posters and the series of tourist signs by Daniel Nebot, Nacho Lavernia and Paco Bascuñán, which for once avoided the use of pictograms.

Again, the larger commissions undertaken by La Nave came from public institutions rather than private enterprise. As a flexible, multi-disciplinary studio, La Nave responded to local demands, pulling in work at a national and international level as it developed its reputation. As already suggested, while local public institutions understandably preferred to employ local designers, the few large corporate retail and commercial concerns tended to use the expertise of multinational or foreign consultancies. Conversely, smaller indigenous studios could handle the smaller commissions.

Through the 1980s, larger Spanish design consultancies were developed. Like La Nave, these came about by studios and individual designers merging, having discovered their frequent joint interest in projects. Other than this, there was little in common between them.

The first consultancy to specialize in corporate identity was Taula de Disseny, formed by Josep Mª Civit in Barcelona in 1981. Its main task was to gain the credibility of companies, to win them away from reliance on foreign consultan-

Corporate identity for Raventos i Blanc, cava company
Taula de Disseny
1988
Towards the end of the 1980s, many food and wines companies made a particularly strong export drive. As part of this trend, a modern image was sought by companies such as Raventos i Blanc.

cies offering this service. Coming from a background in communication marketing, Civit was already well linked to potential clients. Within a few months of opening, Taula de Disseny gained its most important and visible commission, that of the designing the applications (interiors, stationery, publicity and so on) for Landor Associates' new logo for the savings bank 'La Caixa'. At the time, 'La Caixa' was Catalonia's most important bank and, with the merger with La Caixa de Barcelona in 1989, it became Spain's strongest bank. Through the 1980s Taula de Disseny grew from twelve to between twenty and thirty professionals, making it one of the largest studios by Spanish standards. As its name suggests, Taula de Disseny (design table) aimed to bring together individuals around common projects. In this way, it could be quite fluid, often bringing in designers for particular jobs: Civit's vocation was to unite many disparate studios in order to create a strength to compete with the increasing interventions of foreign groups.

Developing at the same time, but in a different direction, was Arcadi Moradell y Asociados. Arcadi Moradell created his own studio at the age of 19 in 1969. With the advantage that his father had a graphic design studio, he had the confidence to move towards larger-scale projects, by 1980 being responsible for the re-designing of the corporate image of Madrid's Metro system. From 1983 AMA centred itself around management and design of the corporate image, picking up increasingly prestigious accounts, including the Caixa de Barcelona. Petrocat and the hotels chain, Grupo Sol. It also opened new offices in Madrid and Seville, as well as Barcelona.

It is noteworthy that, as AMA consolidated its work for large enterprises in the face of growing foreign competition, at the same time it opened up in 1989 a new line specializing in corporate identity packages created in only fifteen days for small- and middle-sized companies. Thus it recognized these sectors as important and innovatory entities in the Spanish economy and was continually interested in decentralizing its business activities to exploit different opportunities. This new line produced very cheap identity programmes for companies unwilling or unable to invest in expensive, complex redesign packages: an appropriate answer to the situation. Likewise, other larger studios, such as that of C R Design & Communication, worked with all types of clients. Although it had a staff of 30, with offices in Barcelona and Madrid, its director Carlos Rolando exerted a powerful influence on its design, in particular in the strong use of typography. This influence applied to the Seville Expo '92 logo, as well as to smaller commissions, such as clothing labels.

The manoeuvrability conceded to the few larger Spanish design groups by being 'on-site', compared with foreign enterprises which relied on an agent or their own administrative offices, gave them a particular advantage. Most were

PetroCat

open to the possibility of 'joint ventures' with foreign companies in the late 1980s. However, none was particularly interested in being bought up by the foreign competition. This was partly a reflection of their own confidence. Despite a relatively short period in the business of dealing with larger-scale accounts, these groups experienced little competition among themselves, since they were involved in diverse approaches to the discipline. They were deeply aware of the problems they faced, the biggest of which were the lack of awareness in education and commerce of the need for design management and a lack of experience in marketing design. They were equally aware of their own merits, knowing they could turn their newness to their advantage, offering a fresh, flexible and distinctive approach to corporate identity which could be exported in the 1990s.

Only three agencies, MMLB, Ricardo Pérez and Lorente y Mussons, were purely Spanish. A fourth, Contrapunto, sold a 27 per cent share to BBDO Worldwide in 1988 and, like the other three, made increasing gains in the 1980s against the established dominance of, for example, Bassat Ogilvy & Mather and McCann Erickson. Their most popular and effective advertising campaign was carried out for TV España, focusing on a young boy who is the object of a tug-of-love between the television and the attention of his best friend, a German

Corporate identity for PetroCat, petroleum company
Arcadi Moradell y Asociados
1988
The petroleum industry underwent changes of organization during the 1980s. Its economic base began to change, too: for instance, whereas only 40 per cent of the income of other European petrol companies came from the actual sale of petrol (the rest coming from services, accessories, etc.), in Spain petrol represented 90 per cent of income. This situation was bound to be challenged and a new corporate identity programme would have to reflect the altered market.

shepherd dog. The aim of TV España was to persuade the viewer to 'learn to use the television well'. Such a campaign reflected in no small way an awareness of the fine balance between quantity and quality in visual communication.

While Spain's development in the 1980s brought about a whole new range of new images, there was none the less a consciousness in many quarters of the damage that sign-saturation – through excessive television watching, advertising or even design – might have. Institutions were no doubt looking over their shoulders to the effects of the economic development ('at all costs') of the 1960s, with its uncontrolled spreading of unsophisticated, vulgar publicity. It was little surprise that in the late 1980s the central government set about systematically dismantling the vast billboards which had flanked Spain's major roads for several decades. New, more cultivated and refined levels for graphic expression had been discovered.

Opposite, top: Daily newspaper, *Diari de Barcelona* 1987-88
Satué's energetic and innovatory leanings were fulfilled in designing this Catalan newspaper. Each day the colour emblem was designed by a different artist or designer.

Bottom, left to right: Emblems by Mariscal 1987, Robert Llimós 1987, Miguel Barceló 1987.

Narrativa en llengua catalana

Narrativa en llengua castellana

Poesia en llengua catalana

Poesia en llengua castellana

Mitjans de Comunicació

Arts escèniques

Cinema

Arts plàstiques

Música simfònica o de càmera

Música moderna i jazz

Història de Barcelona

"Agustí Duran i Sanpere"

Investigació

Restauració d'edificis

Arquitectura i urbanisme

Left: Poster for Ajuntament de Barcelona prizes
Josep Bagà
1989

Above: Magazine, *L'Home Invisible*
Josep Bagà
1989

The tendency for graphic designers, such as Bagà, to work individually — rather than in larger studios — results invariably in their working on diverse projects.

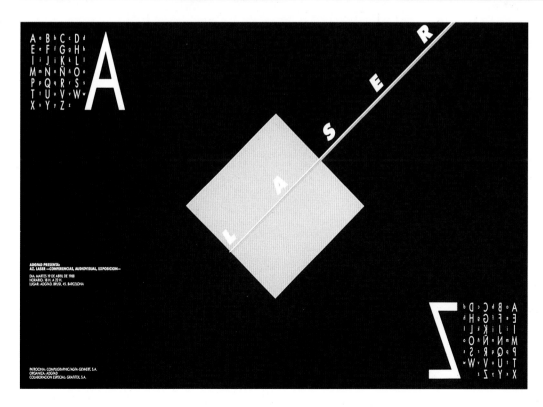

Above left and right: Posters for
Zeleste bar events
Guillem Vidal
1988
The 1980s saw a blossoming of
work for cultural events, both on
the night-circuit of bars and for
formal administrative bodies. This
in turn encouraged a vigorous,
painterly style, which was
sometimes brought to more
commercial work.

Right: Publicity for A-Z Laser
computer graphics system seminar
Albert Isern
1988
Like Satué and many Spanish
designers of all disciplines in his
generation, Isern was profoundly
affected by the events of the late
1960s, which eventually allowed a
break from Swiss-influenced
ideologies to much greater
eclecticism in the use of images
and typography.

Left: Poster for cava festival in Sant Sadurni d'Anoia
Peret
1989

Above: Image used in poster for Biennial exhibition in Barcelona
Peret
1985

Opposite, top left: Poster for Disseny a Palma exhibition
Peret
1989

Opposite, bottom left: Logo for Zsa Zsa bar
Peret
1988

Opposite, far right: Poster for Grec '88 cultural festival in Barcelona
Peret
1988

Radical and controversial elements in Peret's work helped rather than hindered him in obtaining commissions from the Barcelona city council, who aimed to present a young image. Peret's painterly approach encompassed various styles, ranging from Constructivism to Figurative Expressionism. Sometimes such themes as the Pan for the Grec posters recur, but they are always treated in different ways.

disseny a Palma

Left: Shopping bags for Vinçon shop
Pati Nuñez
1989
Vinçon lettering by América Sánchez, 1972. In the summer of 1989, Catalan TV3 showed and advertisement for Vinçon, in which Fernando Amat asks how much it costs to put an advertisement on TV3. In hearing the reply, he exclaims: 'But we can't spend that, we've only just changed the bags!'

Below: Software packaging for CTA S.A.
Josep Mª Trias, Quod Diseño y Marketing
1988

Right: Symbol for the Barcelona '92 Olympic Games
Josep Mª Trias, Quod Diseño y Marketing
1988

Two distinct tendencies in Spanish graphic design of the late 1980s were the influences of Neville Brody (to be seen in Pati Nuñez, among others) and Miró (assumed in some of the work of Josep MªTrias). In thè case of each designer, however, these only represented one of many facets.

Barcelona'92

Jocs de la XXVa Olimpíada
Barcelona 1992

Juegos de la XXV Olimpíada
Barcelona 1992

Jeux de la XXVe Olympiade
Barcelona 1992

Games of the XXV Olympiad
Barcelona 1992

Above: Cover of *Víbora* comic, no. 8-9
Mariscal
1980
Víbora heading by América Sánchez, 1979

Above right: Cover of *El Sidecar* comic
Mariscal
1976
Iniciativas Editoriales

Right: T-shirt
Mariscal
1984
Produced by Dos i Una

Right: Poster for Duplex bar in Cánovas, Valencia
Mariscal
1980

Mariscal's sketchy, angular style, developed in comic drawing from the early 1970s, was subsequently transferred to all types of design work, from T-shirts, to fabrics, to the 1992 Olympic mascot. His background in comics has been a major influence in keeping graphic design colourful and humorous.

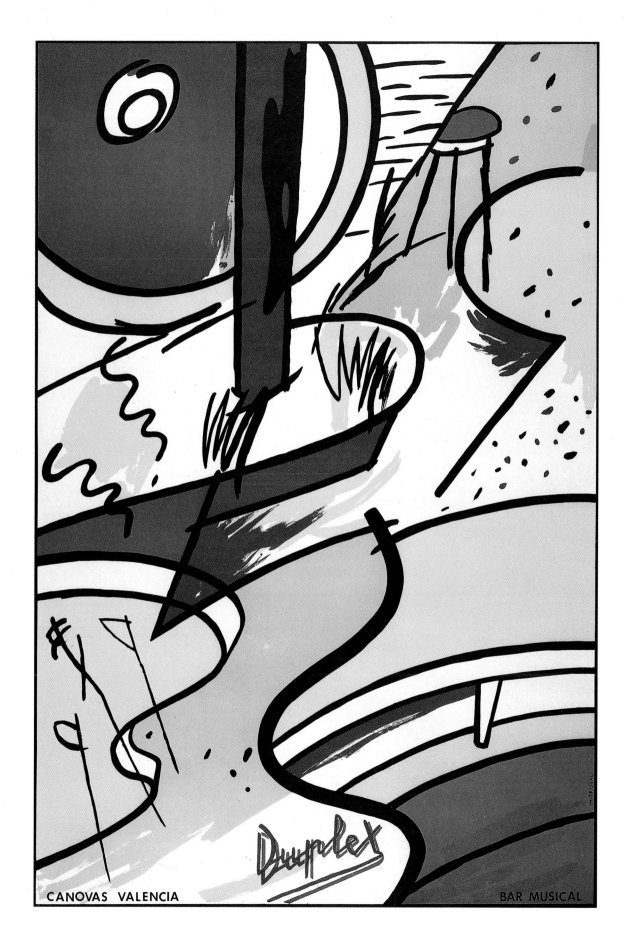

CANOVAS VALENCIA

BAR MUSICAL

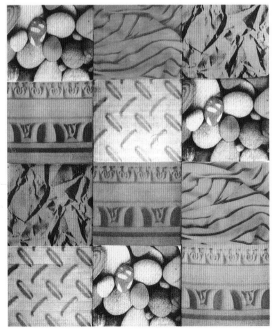

Above left: Sheets and duvet for Castilla Textil
Sandra Figuerola and Marisa Gallén
1989

Far left: Packaging for dismantleable swimming
pool for TOI
Sandra Figuerola and Marisa Gallén
1989

Left: Writing pad for Don Antonio
Sandra Figuerola and Marisa Gallén
1988

Above: Sign system for Valencia bus company, CVT
(Consorcio Valenciano de Transportes)
Paco Bascuñán
1986

Above: Poster for music-bar, De Naranjas
Luís González
1985

Right: Poster for Salón de Diseñadores,
Feria de la Moda Infantíl
Luís González
1987

Three hours south of Barcelona and one hour
north of Benidorm, Valencia acts outside
Catalan cultural traditions but none the less
brings a sunny, if sometimes anarchic
freshness to design, as exhibited in the work
of members of La Nave.

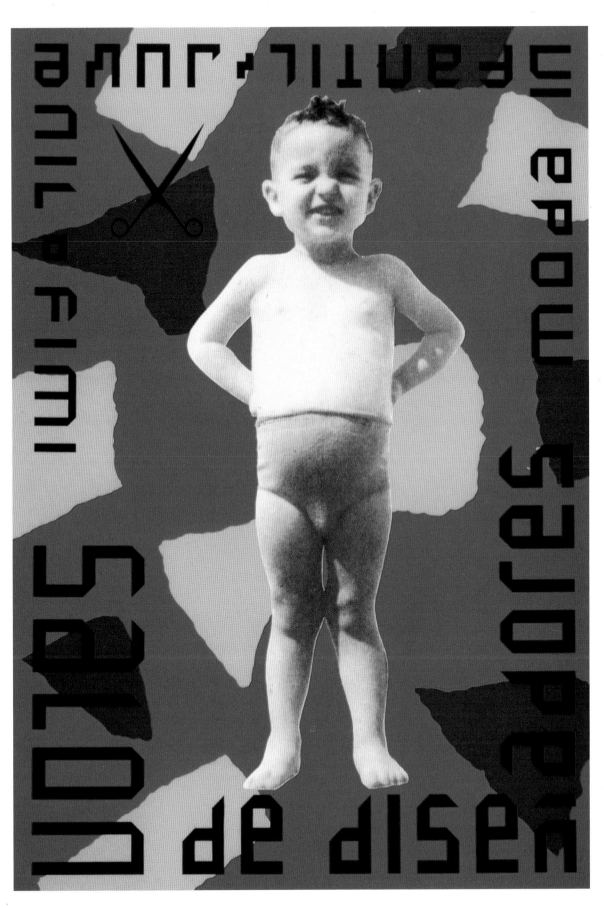

Above: Poster for Camper shoes, 'The Camper Trail'
Carlos Rolando
1987

Right: Poster for Camper shoes, 'Spring'
Carlos Rolando
1987

Far right: Publicity for Sevilla '92 Expo
Carlos Rolando
1988

Carlos Rolando (formerly of Rolando & Memelsdorff Asociados, now CR Design and Communication Services) demonstrates that visual energy is not lost in the context of one of Spain's largest graphic design studios. Tandem's tourist logo — bottom right — is a good example of Miróism.

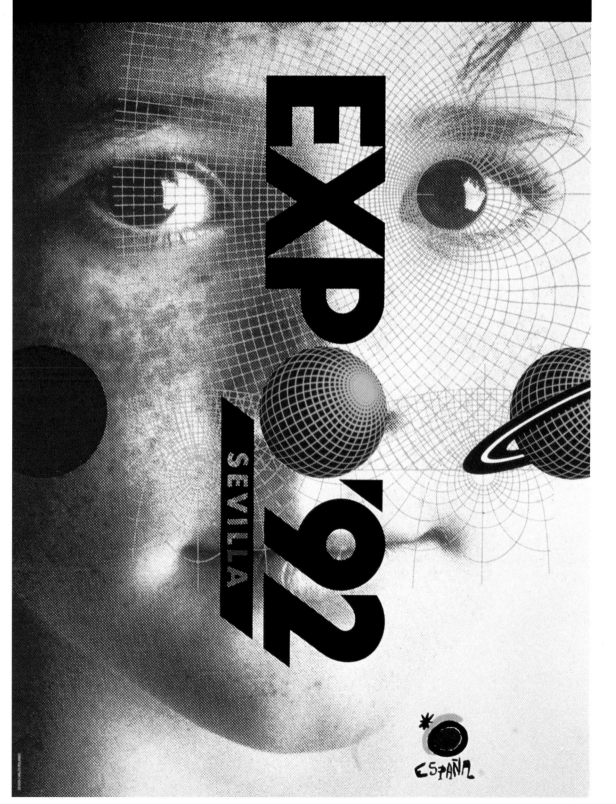

EXPOSICION UNIVERSAL
DE SEVILLA 1992

20 DE ABRIL A
12 DE OCTUBRE DE 1992

EXP

SEVILLA

'92

ESPAÑA

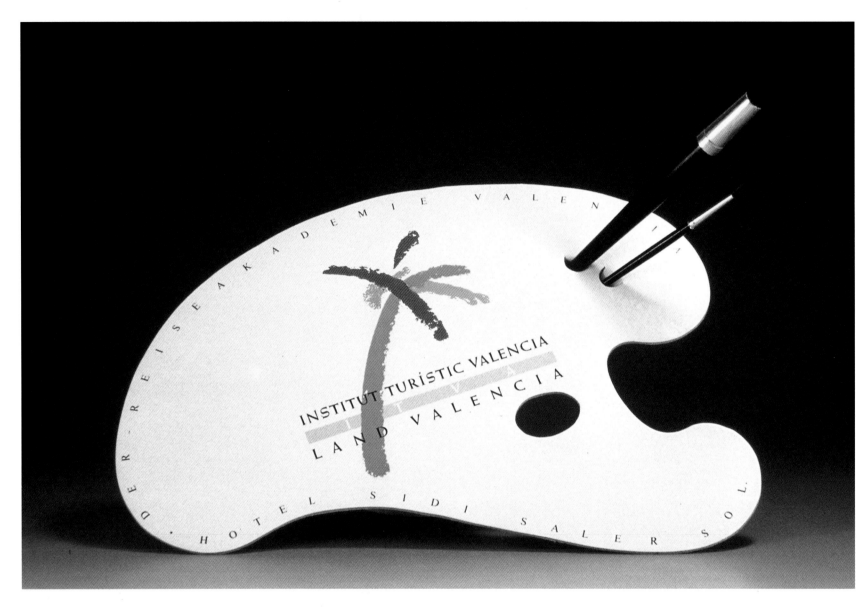

Tourist logo for Valencia Region
Pepe Gimeno with Paco Buscuñán
1987
Administrative reorganization in Spain required its
re-design as well. Designers such as Pepe Gimeno
came out of advertising agencies to set up graphic
design studios benefiting from the industrial and
administrative reconversion of Spain.

Advertisement for Radio Televisión España:
Aprende a usar la televisión (learn to use the
television)
Contrapunto
1988
Contrapunto, one of Spain's largest and most
potent advertising agencies, showed its strengths
against foreign competition with leading
advertising campaigns.

4

interiors and public spaces

New Modernism and Modernistic Baroque

d ESIGN FOR THE PUBLIC DOMAIN DURING the 1980s was a challenging, but precarious exercise in Spain. In the renovation of the urban landscape, old buildings had to be restored, but new forms also had to be created to fill the waste grounds left by Francoism. A brighter past and a new future both had to be represented. If parks and plazas were to be used by all, they should not alienate any group of their users. Neither were they expendable as, say, a piece of unpopular graphic design: doing away with a new park is a costly exercise. New bars or shops were in a slightly different position, for customers could at least vote with their feet (and in many cases, they did). Nevertheless, in both interiors and urban spaces, design came under greater public scrutiny than in other areas.

In Barcelona this was a particularly intense process – as, fortunately, was the animation behind the projects. Indeed, through the phenomena of the urban spaces and bars, a particular strain of Spanish design – known by its Catalan denomination, *disseny* – was identified with Barcelona. This was in recognition of its strength, but also of the fastidiousness afforded it by the designers and the demands made of it by the public. For various reasons these interiors, together with the public spaces, belong more to design than to architecture or planning. Firstly, they were conceived as projects rather than schemes, or plans; secondly, they are accessible (not all architecture is accessible to everybody); thirdly, many of the parks and plazas are subject more to a sculptural than to a constructional approach; fourthly, for historical reasons, Spain demonstrated a fluid movement of professionals between architecture and design.

During the 1980s, Spain began to produce architecture of major significance, but historically many architects had involved themselves in all aspects of design, especially in their preoccupation for their immediate environment. The 'urban concern' was an issue at the centre of discussion amongst avant-garde architects in the bars and cafés of Barcelona during the *dictatura*. Physically, Barcelona – a

Opposite: Velvet bar, Barcelona, entrance
Alfredo Arribas
1987

city lodged between mountains and sea – has always encountered problems of space and structure.

A visionary plan, the 'Eixample' (or 'Ensanche' in Castilian), had been made by Ildefons Cerdà in 1859. This fixed a grid system which would extend the city far beyond its medieval walls. However, as it was developed from the late

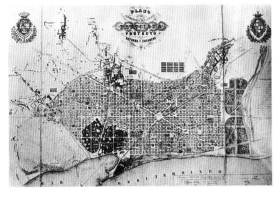

nineteenth century, it touched into surrounding towns, such as Gràcia, Sant Gervasi, Sants and Les Corts, and the problem of their incorporation was not foreseen. Whilst solutions were sought via Léon Jaussely's 1903 plan to impose a total unity of design on the city, through GATCPAC's collaboration with Le Corbusier to produce the 'Macià' plan in 1934, demographic change constantly exacerbated the problem. This became particularly acute in the 1950s and 60s with the massive influx of immigrants from other parts of Spain, particularly the South, the consequence of which were larger *barracas* (shanty towns) and the throwing up of satellite suburbs, such as Hospitalet de Llobregat.

Above: The Pla Cerdà, 1859, devised by Ildefons Cerdà, destined to provide a blueprint for the urban development of Barcelona for the next 150 years by the development of the grid system called Eixample (Catalan) or Ensanche (Castilian).

In 1980, following the first democratic city council elections since the 1930s, Oriol Bohigas was appointed as Director of Public Works under a socialist administration. In an economic recession, private commissions had stopped and the onus was on public building – schools and sports facilities, libraries and hospitals for the regional government, the Generalitat and the city council, the Ajuntament. After years of neglect, it was clear that the general urban fabric of Barcelona had to be addressed as well. However, unlike previous occasions, the answer under Bohigas was to conceive the urban renovation in terms of projects rather than a grand master plan. By this stage, the latter approach would have been inappropriate. The city's demographic expansion had stabilized, so massive housing schemes were not required. The wide boulevards provided by Cerdà's 1859 plan still allowed reasonable circulation. Thus new motorway arteries to link or unclog different parts were not of primary importance. What was required, though, was a change of emphasis within the city. Barcelona's old centre was heavily loaded with the connotations of city centre; the suburbs, on the other hand, were devoid of meaning, their incorporation into the growing city being matched by their neglect. To bring both cohesion to the city's parts, as well as to give each *barrio* dignity and character, urban renewal was to work from the particular to the general.

This attitude had been somewhat prefigured and aided by the Plan General Metropolitano of 1976. Its formulation had been influenced by the infiltration of various professionals into the town planning department. Under the conditions afforded by the political opening up of late-Francoism, they were able to

Right: Pavement tiles, Barcelona
Antoni Gaudí
Hijo de E.F. Escofet S.A. since
1960
Designed 1904-06

Far right: BM street lamp
Iron tubing
Pep Bonet and Miguel Milà
Diseño Ahorro Energetico for
Polinax
1967
Hijo de E.F. Escofet S.A and Diseño
Ahorro Energetico S.A.
increasingly established
themselves from the 1960s
onwards as Spain's most
innovatory producers of urban
furniture and paving.

suggest a more radical way of tackling the 'urban concern'. The subsequent economic and political instabilities did not allow this plan to be carried through, but it was important in reserving Barcelona's few remaining open spaces for the development of parks and plazas, as well as more generally in bringing the concept of working by projects rather than plans into play. At the same time, it also represented a shift towards the reinforcement and reinterpretation of pre-existing architectural identities. A letter had been published in 1965 in *La Vanguardia* and signed by many important figures of the Modern Movement, including Le Corbusier, Nikolaus Pevsner, Gio Ponti and Alexandre Cirici. This called for the preservation of the authentic Gaudí legacy, which was being eroded by the uncontrolled and scantily considered 'restoration' of the Sagrada Família, and also implied that the proper re-use (without pastiche) of antique buildings could act in the urban development of the city.

The ideas for urban renewal therefore had a long pedigree. In anticipation of the large volume of work, some commentators in the late 1970s saw this as a platform for the establishment of a second 'Escuela de Barcelona' after its debacle earlier in the decade. Many of its original members were involved in the programmes. Correa-Milà worked on the Plaça Real and later directed work on the Olympic installations on Montjuïc. Oscar Tusquets and Lluís Clotet worked on the old quarter of Raval. Bohigas's own studio, MBM, was to work on the Olympic Village and its accompanying redevelopment, in line with Cerdà's plan, in the Poble Nou area to the north of the city. But with over 100 projects under way in this scheme, the net was spread wider. By the time it came to be im-

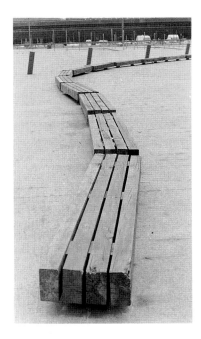

Above and opposite: Plaça dels Països Catalans, Barcelona
Helio Piñón and Albert Viaplana
1983
While its forms make reference to its immediate railway station setting (l'Estació de Sants), this plaza also invokes the language of Minimalism as a viable expression. In the background can be seen Andres Nagel's sculpture and a tower of the adjoining Parc de l'Espanya Industrial.

plemented under Bohigas in the early 1980s, there existed a substantial pool of younger architects influenced by him or by the important figure Rafael Moneo. Their influence was found in an interest in history, a sensitive eclecticism and an attention to detail. While the responses to each problem were visually diverse, in the individual treatment of each problem, and in the plays on language – whether the established language of Modernism or of Modernisme – unifying solutions were found.

The most ambitious scheme was the development of three parks around the main railways station of Sants. The first of these to be completed, in 1983, was Helio Piñón's and Albert Viaplana's Plaça dels Països Catalans. The rhomboidal space it occupied was awkward: it was bounded by busy streets, isolating it from the immediate surrounding architecture; straddling the sunken railway tracks, it could not take more trees or buildings. The solution appeared as a dialogue of Modernist suggestions, with modest lines stretching across a clear, rectilinear grid set up by the paving. There is little purely functional about this plaça, though: there are no children's swings, drinking fountains or clearly marked out meeting points. Instead, the whole space acts as an enormous sculpture in which the observer plays a part as he moves through it. Two mesh roofs supported by thin poles, one tall and cuboid, the other low and sweeping, push the space upward and outward. Meanwhile, they are punctuated by smaller elements around them, such as inclined poles, which at night wash pools of light across

the paving. The whole area was designed to function both day and night, the shadows of the canopies drifting across the ground during the day, and the night lighting picking out the structure as well as creating a glowing ground.

On first examination, the plaça seems purely abstract in its conception. However, a suppressed narrative slowly reveals itself. One begins to find plinths without statues, advertising hoardings without posters, a cascading fountain without bowls. In the creation of a large concourse with points of references, the artefacts and life of its immediate railway station setting are invoked by only the slightest suggestion. In fact, the scenarios of each part, or in other words its narrative, only served as a tool for its architects in conceiving the project; the rest has to be discovered by reading and interracting with the signs left behind. In playing with the language of Modernism, at both an abstract level and a symbolic level, Piñón and Viaplana produced a lyrical Minimalist essay which ensured its revival as a viable aesthetic beyond Postmodernism.

More accessible to all – and in that respect, more Postmodern – was a baroque, almost beserk and certainly polemical solution for the Parc de l'Espanya Industrial by the Santander architect, Luis Peña-Ganchegui, completed in 1985. Situated on the other side of the Sants station, it has surreal, lighthouse-like belvedere towers, fountain jets and football terrace leading down to a pool for pleasure boats: Peter Buchanan's description – 'a mixture of Disney and Gaudí' – is apt. Now it also incorporates a sports hall, while, at its other end, a vast sculpture by Andres Nagel of St George's Dragon (St George is patron saint of Catalonia) doubles as a children's slide. If the experience of Piñón and Viaplana's Plaça dels Països Catalans is almost ethereal, activity in Peña's park is more direct, for it is conceived almost like a fun park, perhaps partly because its planning was undertaken in conjunction with the city council and the local neighbourhood association.

The trilogy of parks around the Sants station is completed by the Parc de l'Escorxador, occupying four blocks of the original Cerdà grid. It was commissioned by competition in 1981, the winning scheme to be accompanied by a series of Joan Miró sculptures. Ricardo Bofill's entry included a classical temple which (according to Oriol Bohigas's autobiography) Miró described as antiquated and dehumanized, like the last inheritance of Francoism. Wherever Bofill's Postmodern classicism coincided with the Imperial style of Francoist architecture the results would rarely find favour in Modern Barcelona.

The winning entry was designed by Andreu Arriola, Beth Galí, Màrius Quintana and Antoni Solanas. It provided a parcelling up of the large, flat space into different areas of activity which could be completed in phases. The unfortunate death of Miró during the development of this project meant that the proposed 'forest of sculptures' was never realized. They were planned in ceramic and were

Opposite: Sculpture of St George's Dragon
Andres Nagel
1985
Doubling as a slide, this sculpture introduces the fun-park scheme of the Parc de l'Espanya Industrial.

to provide pieces which could be touched and climbed over and inside. What did survive to installation was Miró's tall *Woman and Bird* sculpture, set in a square pond. In a development of his mural at the airport and medallion in the paving near the docks, this one symbolized a gateway to the city by land. Criticism levelled at this park suggested that it provided a confused reading between the spaces. Needless to say, however, the incorporation of the last work of the ubiquitously popular Miró in a new park situated on the old site of Barcelona's abattoir could not but have symbolized a rebirth for the city.

The completion of these three parks provided new points of reference for the city whilst also linking Sants right down to the Plaça d'Espanya. At the other end of Barcelona a smaller project revitalized the Avinguda Gaudí, which sliced diagonally through the Cerdà plan, linking Gaudí's Sagrada Família with Domènech i Muntaner's Hospital de Sant Pau. To join these two masterpieces of Modernista architecture, light fittings by Pere Falques for the 1888 exhibition were brought out of storage and re-used, linking the spire of each building with its own finial. Between them, Màrius Quintana and the Barcelona council's Servei de Projectes Urbans placed a staccato of benches, metal balls, kiosks and pergolas which created a visual continuity along the pedestrianized street without crowding it out.

The sensitive placing of urban furniture and other features almost acted as a microcosm of the overall philosophy of this type of urban renewal. In the Avinguda Gaudí, historical elements were used appropriately without sapping the life out of them by ill-considered pastiche. They interplayed with Modernist forms, which in themselves were subject to a poetic treatment. Each furnishing was considered in its context, while at the same time propagating a unity through the overall project.

Within this scheme of projects, other notable interventions included the Plaça del Sol by Jaume Bach and Gabriel Mora, completed in 1985. The square was one of nine new developments in the old town of Gràcia, of which Bach and Mora worked on four. Their experience as teaching assistants to Rafael Moneo and Oriol Bohigas and in working with Piñón and Viaplana helps to explain the close attention to detail and elegant, sensitive response to the space. The Plaça del Sol is a clear space with an expansive pavement over a subterranean car park flanked on one side by three poles providing reflecting lights, and on the other by a long canopy into which a footbridge comes in at an angle, over the ramp to the car park.

Refurbishment of squares took place throughout Catalonia, more often than not exhibiting the same clarity and control. An exception may lie in a work by Enric Miralles, who had collaborated with Piñón and Viaplana in the Sants station plaça and produced, with his wife, Carme Pinós, an even more adventurous square in the town of Parets del Valles. Here the canopies float and inter-weave while being supported by an almost Constructivist system of beams. As the forms apparently fall over each other, then the whole conception appears to teeter on the edge of the ludicrous. Such brinkmanship, however, results in an ebullient articulation of the space.

While the interior of Catalonia was subject to piecemeal renovation, Barcelona not only attended to its squares, parks and courtyards, but also re-opened itself out to the sea. Previously, one would have walked down the famous Ramblas cutting through Barcelona's old quarter, towards the sea, arriving at Gaietà Buigas's 1886 monument to Christopher Columbus, a figure atop a Corinthian column pointing out across the Mediterranean. However, once there, it was no longer possible to follow the call of the sea: a busy road and fenced waste-ground – once used for loading and unloading of shipping – inhibited passage to the water's edge. Many European cities had given up the struggle to orientate their metropolis towards the sea; in Barcelona the question had a symbolic aspect in the sense that the city had historically turned its back on the rest of Spain, preferring a more 'European' orientation.

With the development of the Olympic Village further up the coast, which included beach reclamation (itself starting with the cleaning of the amusingly urban beach of the Barceloneta), the development of jetties and a seafront esplanade, this process was underlined. The anticipated extra traffic between the Olympic Village to the north and the Olympic sporting emplacements on Mont-juïc to the south would pass across the seafront of the port, effectively cutting the city off from the sea even more. A competition for a solution to the area where the city fronted onto the port, called the Moll de la Fusta, was won by Manuel de Solà-Morales. He proposed, firstly, that the road running along the port front from the Columbus monument was sunk, allowing free access for pedestrians over it and down to the water's edge. Two decks, one half covering the road, and the other beyond it at the water's edge, were joined by pedestrian bridges which, with their cantilevered raising mechanism, recall port emplacements. The water-front area was planted with regular rows of trees, providing an extensive walk-way, where in addition cultural events might take place (including the presenta-tion of the Olympic flag to Barcelona in 1988). Overlooking the walkway on the higher deck, six *chiringuitos* (seaside huts) house a range of bars, cafés and restaurants, which was a prerequisite of the plans. Manuel de Solà-Morales's *chiringuitos*, which opened in 1988, were constructed with a curved roof to resemble a vast wave coming in from the sea and crashing over the rocks which make up their walls.

The interior design of each was carried out by a different group, the most spectacular result being El Gambrinus by the architect Alfredo Arribas working

Above: Bridge connecting the two decks of the Moll de la Fusta and spanning the sunken waterfront road, Barcelona
Manuel de Solà-Morales
1986

with Mariscal. This tapas bar was conceived as an epic film script. The inside was developed as the interior of a transatlantic liner, with clean, elegant lines. The windows were frosted and engraved with weed and sea creatures, however, to give an underwater effect. The exterior terrace then continues the story to the effect that the ship has sunk and the survivors have put together the wreckage to furnish it. Thus, no chair is the same; some are encrusted with octopuses and shellfish of pure Mariscal creation. The parasols are weatherbeaten. On the roof of El Gambrinus a vast prawn rides the wave; since the bar is situated at the end of the Moll de la Fusta, the sea creature is intended as an irreverent counterpoint to the Columbus monument.

In the urban design of El Gambrinus and the accompanying setting of the Moll de la Fusta, Barcelona's relationship to the sea was recaptured. The rebuilding of Mies van der Rohe's 1929 Pavilion in 1986 in turn helped recapture her relationship with a lost history. The original pavilion was built to represent Germany in Barcelona's Exhibition of 1929, a time when Barcelona was also at a pinnacle of economic and cultural strength. Although ephemeral, the pavilion has consistently been quoted ever since as a torchbearing example of the Modern Movement. Its rebuilding had been suggested as far back as 1957 when the Grup R approached Mies with the idea. Subsequent attempts to revive the idea in the 1960s and 1970s also petered out. During the so-called 'Bohigas years' of the early 1980s, when Oriol Bohigas was placed in charge of town planning and building, the scheme was carried through.

Initially it became known mostly through black and white photographs, but when the rebuilding was completed under the direction of Cristian Cirici, Fernando Ramos and Ignasi de Solà-Morales, the full richness of the design, particularly in its coloured marble facing, became apparent to both tourists and locals alike. Again it demonstrated that a sensuous, expressive Modernism was possible.

At the time, the rebuilding not only signified the symbolic recovery of Modernism in Spain, but also signalled attitudes which are found elsewhere in Barcelona design: once again, Barcelona was a historical seat for radical design proposals. The result of rebuilding the pavilion was to make permanent an ephemeral piece of architecture; what had been an expression of its time took on a new solidity. Thus the appropriation of a past aesthetic was legitimated. While copious research was undertaken to ensure a faithful reproduction of the original building, its very reconstruction lay it open to reinterpretations in terms of its meaning. Previously emblematic of the German contribution to an international exhibition, it was now an object of tourism.

These attitudes, and in particular shifts between the ephemeral and the solid, were echoed in many new interiors. Barcelona saw another spectacular and unparalleled innovation in the 1980s connected with an architecture-related design discipline: the *bares de diseño*, otherwise known as the *bares modernos*, or the *bares frios*. Such was the strength and popularity of these bars that they virtually became a design movement in their own right. Certain parts of town, and certain types of bars in Barcelona had always gone in and out of fashion. In the late 1960s, Tuset Street, a close re-creation of London's Carnaby Street, was in vogue. In the late 1970s and early 1980s the rowdier atmosphere of the carrer Ample in the old city was the most frequented. And as the 1980s progressed, a more *chic* line in bars – concentrated along the upper end of the Diagonal – came to prominence. Each new bar had to be more perfect that the last.

While the transformation of bars emphasized their ephemeral nature, the emblematic weight they carried in the public imagination meant that they became lasting statements of designerly intention. In other words, while many bars were subject to frequent re-designing, each time they were treated with such care that their image would live beyond their life. The rebuilding of the Mies van der Rohe pavilion in its way represented a similar crossover between the ephemeral and the permanent.

Much of Barcelona design was perceived and understood through these bars: each new one was anticipated with excitement. Therefore, the names of their designers became known, too. The popularity of the *bares de diseño* may be explained by the disproportion between spending power and taste that existed in the 1980s. Interior designer Jordi Bieto described this as follows in 1987: 'On the one hand, there is a sector with great acquisitive power, but with a very classical taste. And on the other hand, there is the young, without great acquisitive power, but with a great desire for innovation. This last group cannot commission interesting projects from interior designers individually, and the other group doesn't want to. Thus the bars carry out such an important function.' By paying a bit more for a drink, one could sit on a Transatlantic stool or a Carlos Riart chair without actually having to buy them.

The bars' popularity may also be more simply explained by the fact that much more of social life in Spain takes place outside the home, and thus in restaurants and bars, than in, for example, northern Europe. This is not to say that in other cities of Spain, people didn't go out at night. Far from it. Nearly every city and town in Spain boasts its particular *marcha*, its relentless nightlife, especially and justifiably, Madrid and Valencia. Nevertheless, there was not yet to be found the pedigree of perfected modern design applied to commercial spaces in these cities as there was in Barcelona. When commenting on their own El Gambrinus, Mariscal and Alfredo Arribas suggested that 'In Barcelona, people go out to see each other. In Madrid people go out to meet each other.' In this respect, the stage set had to complement the social interaction.

Above: Flash-Flash restaurant, Barcelona
Alfonso Milà and Frederico Correa
1971
Barcelona's architect-designed bar and café interiors movement has a pedigree which stretches back before the 1980s.

Moreover, the stage set also augmented and manipulated that social interaction. Apart from being fashionable watering-holes, the new bars may also be interpreted within the context of the cultural street life of the city. We have seen how ADIFAD's organization of the 1971 ICSID conference included a *happening* organized by Miralda. The same Miralda plans a wedding ceremony for 1992 between the Christopher Columbus monument and New York's Statue of Liberty to celebrate the five hundredth anniversary of Columbus's voyage. The years between have been peppered with public, artistic-theatrical events. Theatre groups such as 'Els Joglars' and 'Fura dels Baus' built their reputations on street happenings. Bars such as Zeleste and Up and Down also provided spaces for alternative theatrical events. In addition, the school Eina was a regular seat for such events as Xavier Olivé's 'Esculturas al Aire Libre' (1975), in which students used their own bodies to re-create sculptures in the grounds of the school. Artists associated with Eina organized, at the end of 1972, two weeks of conceptual art, *happenings* and performances in the streets of the immigrant satellite town of Hospitalet de Llobregat. The involved participation of people of the town was important, as Alexandre Cirici reflected: 'A growing consciousness of this dramatization of social life has allowed the exercise. . . of considering May 1968 like a vast work of art at a city level, and conversely, makes it difficult to define the parameters of art exhibitions, *happenings*, ceremonies, programmes of ephemeral pieces of communication, whether they are art or real social life. A kind of catharsis was produced which meant that the festival didn't become an evasion. It was actually like a ceremony of freedom.' Participation was therefore an antidote to the public passiveness that the Franco years had engendered in the culture of evasion. Artistic-theatrical events acted as pinpricks to stir the collective imagination.

Of course, Spain has long traditions of theatrical street ceremonies, both religious and non-religious. Barcelona's own *Carrer Foc*, a kind of 'running of the bulls' involving fireworks and devils rather than bulls, underwent a revival after its dampening under Francoism. The intermixing of artistic life and social life spread, in the 1980s, to the modern bars. The sense of 'participation' lived on, albeit in an oblique way, by the patronage of the new scenographies of the *bares de diseño*. It is in this light that the themes and usage of these bars may be read.

Developments in fashion shops on the Passeig de Gràcia and the Rambla de Catalunya had signalled a new direction in interior design which acted in the earlier 1980s as preparatory ground for the bars. They featured close contact between shop proprietor and designer. In fact sometimes, as in the case of Alícia Nuñez of Zig-Zag and Tokyo, owner and designer were the same person. In the early 1980s, Spain still had not come out of the economic crises. In this climate, architects such as Eduardo Samsó coming out of the Escuela de Arquitectura de Barcelona in 1980, found few opportunities in that profession. The fashion business, being more fluid, flexible and even submerged, was able to some extent to revive itself faster. Accordingly, new retail outlets established themselves in an overall recession. Proprietors commissioned exciting and provocative interiors to display their goods. The tendencies were towards playing with the level of geometry, scale, texture and, above all, images. Samsó's Bis de Bis shoe shop (1983) placed shoes close up to the window, floating in space or on the floor – anywhere in fact where one wouldn't normally expect to see them.

A veteran designer whose work in shop interiors became increasingly adventurous during the 1980s was Pepe Cortés. His close work with Mariscal in furniture in which he demonstrated his openness to the most far-fetched, but also effective, propositions was echoed in his interior work. While the interior of A/2, a fashion shop in Manresa, was being worked on, a large block of bedrock was uncovered; this became the basis for the shop and was partly shaped into steps. Mariscal then provided mock-Ionic decorations for the walls. The interior, completed in 1987, was thus turned into a fictitious archaeological site within which shop fittings and flooring provided another time zone.

A flurry of smaller bars in the mid-1980s paved the way from fashion shop interiors to the larger nocturnal complexes of the later 1980s. These included 33 by Vicente Miranda and Dani Freixa; Snooker by Carlos Riart, Santiago Roqueta, Oleguer Armengol and Victor Mesalles; and Si-si-si and Bijou by Gabriel Ordeig. All demonstrated a habitual reference to the 1940s and 1950s, the use of light as the principal modeller of the space and the inclusion of distorted and sometimes aggressive furnishings.

These bars mostly occupied the ground floors of buildings in the Eixample or Ensanche area of Barcelona. As such, their space was often limited to long, thin units with little scope for experimenting with height. It was, therefore, the potential of the lighting and the richness of furnishing that had to be used to the full.

By contrast, a second league of bars established themselves outside Ensanche in the older towns of Gràcia, Sant Gervasi and Guinardó, occupying buildings which had been small factories or stores. In these larger premises there was more scope for the organization of the internal spaces, and therefore of people. There was also generally a tension created between the creation of clear, austere space and the vibrancy afforded by lighting schemes and detailing, perhaps prefigured by interiors such as those of the famous Paradise in Amsterdam or the lofts of New York.

Above: Jeanne-Pierre Bua fashion shop, Barcelona
Eduardo Samsó
1984
Before moving into bar design in 1985 with Nick Havanna, Samsó had 'cut his teeth' on shop interiors in the earlier 1980s, coinciding with the fashion boom of that period.

In Barcelona itself, to a large extent this concept had been prefigured by Zeleste, opened in 1968 by Silvia Gubern and Angel Jové, the lamp for which we have seen in the chapter on furniture. Zeleste was redesigned in 1980, accentuating this minimalism. The effect was picked up later in Zig-Zag and Otto Zutz (Guillem Bonet, Alícia Nuñez and Jordi Parcerisas), Universal (Claret Serrahima) and KGB (Alfredo Vidal), each one of which achieved it in different ways: Otto Zutz by an industrial setting, for instance; and Universal in slicing up what otherwise might have been a tea room.

Alfredo Arribas and Eduardo Samsó were to push these bars beyond austere minimalism, and introduce greater visual codification. As a designer still in his twenties, Samsó had absorbed an eclectic array of international influences and was also prepared to put into play his observations of everyday life. With the bar Nick Havanna, he took the games of Bis de Bis a step further. Commissioned by competition in 1985, Samsó's Nick Havanna created new limits in attention to detail, coupled with overall concept. In examining the detail, one might start at the toilets, to which Samsó paid particular attention, refusing to treat their function in a simplistic and literal-minded way. Accordingly, he made them larger, less claustrophobic, with urinals as a cascading, mirrored waterfall and the basins almost as shrines. Moving into the main floor of the bar, Samsó provided a wide range of seating and standing arrangements, from the suggestive saddle-like Frenesi stools of Transatlántic around the cow-hide bar (the only strong reference to the fictitious 'Nick Havanna', cowboy conqueror of the West), across the dance floor (standing room only) to the football terraces which overlook a wall of televisions, and beyond them – separated by a glass screen – to a more sumptuous space with leather seating for a more recumbent participation. Each of these reflected the bar's different clientele and/or different stages of one's journey through the evening. Curiosities, such as a pendulum and the subsequent arrival of a pet snake, completed the series of fragmented experiences. In spite of the dense visual text of Nick Havanna, the lighting served to integrate it, bringing (as was intended from the initial conception of the project) the atmosphere of a discotheque to a bar.

If socializing in a bar was to be a visually epic activity in Nick Havanna, then so was eating in Network. The interior work on this café, opened in 1987, was undertaken by Eduardo Samsó with graphic design by Alfons Sostres and Pati Nuñez (as we have already seen). Alfredo Arribas directed the overall project and planned its architectural component. The café was conceived with a script, situating it in a post-nuclear context connected to earlier epochs. Thus Network suggests a vision of the future focused on accumulation, set in a bunker. Television screens poke out from bare concrete walls, while wiring tangles its way along the ceiling, all giving a vision which echoes futuristic films such as Terry

Above: Washrooms, Network café, Barcelona
Alfredo Arribas and Eduardo Samsó
1986
Modernist Baroque or the Postmodern bunker?

Gilliam's *Brasil* and Ridley Scott's *Blade Runner* – indeed, both films were hugely successful in Spain, and were also acknowledged influences on the project. In addition, Samsó, intent on shaping the restaurant as much as a social experience as a gastronomic one, organized the furnishings so that one couldn't avoid eye contact with one's neighbours (and attendant conversations): the television screens were placed so that one had to look across someone else's table to see them, single people were placed directly opposite each other and a vast triangular table was included for large parties. So successful was this social engineering in the early days of Network, that – as customers mixed so easily, moving from one table to another – it became difficult for the waiters to keep up with the movement and get the bills right.

Taking its theme from David Lynch's film, *Blue Velvet*, Velvet (1987), a bar which represented a reaction against the 'Onda fria' (cold wave) of previous bars, was designed by Alfredo Arribas. Here, a ramp led one down to a warm interior of succulent colours. The mixing of the sensuous and the Modernist was brought to an epic, cinematic climax in Arribas's entertainment complex, Louie Vega, situated in Calafell, near Tarragona. Here, a cocktail of baroque and modern exuberance tumbles over 3,000 square metres of terrain. It is small wonder that in 1989, shortly after its completion, Arribas was working in Japan on the ambitious Il Palazzo Hotel in Fukuoka. Not only was Barcelona design known through its bars within the small, dense space of the city: its photographability for international magazines and its promise of memorable nights for the modern tourist carried news of it far.

Where there is great concentration on a particular design activity – as there was in Barcelona – standards may be pushed up by the competition, or they may drop as cliques fall into mannerisms. The ripples from the centre of a movement, however, may be picked up outside and combined with the freshness allowed by that same distancing.

The concentration of new bars and shops in Barcelona made developments into hot, local news, though it must be said that around these first-division bars, a halo of lesser-known bars of varying quality was to be found. Meanwhile, the euphoria of *disseny* was to be picked up in some impressive examples in other cities of Spain. In Seville, Ernesto de Ceano produced bold sweeps of colour and form to cut across the cool interiors of the bars Antenna and Bestiario. The Basque designer, J.A. Beranoagirre, provided weird distortions in the Bilbao shoe shop, Pisazapatos, and the Madrid fashion shop, Trucco. Still in Madrid, Patrocinio Soriano and Mariano del Olmo carried the Capote Club into the twenty-second century, with Vogon-inspired fittings and lighting. Perhaps the last of these demonstrates how Spanish youth culture may depart far from the more serious intentions embodied in most of Barcelona's parks. Set geographically and generationally far away from Barcelona, Capote Club reflects the designers' youthful (both were under 30) openness to different influences to be found in films and magazines, pastiching an optimistic, fun-filled view of the 1950s.

The diffusion of Spain's new bars movement in no small way reflects how spare time is taken seriously. For a nation which takes care over how it dresses itself before going out into the street, appropriately finished interiors were demanded for the important business of socializing. It is often observed that not even the Spanish are quite sure when they sleep; with the long working day in Spain and the late evening meal, much of social life will take place in the small hours. Thus the bars became the scenarios for the normal or dramatic participation of the young in collective life, just as the new parks and plazas became the spaces for all at any time of the day.

It is also quipped that Spanish design in the 1980s had so much *movimiento* that it could not sleep and had to live twenty-four hours a day. Hence the attention played by proprietors and designers to the interiors of their nightspots. The major aesthetic aim in these bars was to differentiate rather than to re-create types. While El Gambrinus or Nick Havanna had their particular narratives, they never formed anything like an orchestrated Disneyesque Theme Bar genre ('. . .and now onto the next glass of hyperreality'). Ultimately, the bars were backdrops for experience, not experiences in themselves. Certainly, as already stated, in their attention to detail, distortions, use of light as the principal factor in describing space, their ironic references to the modernity of the 50s and their good humour, they manifest similarities. In revitalizing and pushing the language of Modernism further they struck chords with the new parks and plazas. And, most important of all, this demonstration that design for the public domain could be avant-garde, challenging, provocative and then accepted lends credence to the aims formulated within the Modern Movement.

Opposite
Top left: Avinguda de Gaudí, Barcelona, shelter
Màrius Quintana and Servei de Projectes Urbans, Ajuntament de Barcelona
1986

Top right: Parc de L'Escorxador, Barcelona
Antoni Solanas, Andreu Arriola, Beth Galí, Màrius Quintana
1987
Conceived originally as a sculpture park for ceramic works by Miró. In the event, because of his death, only Woman and Bird — seen here — was installed.

Bottom left and right: Plaça del Sol, Barcelona
Jaume Bach and Gabriel Mora
1985

Parc de l'Espanya Industrial, Barcelona
Luís Peña Ganchequi and Francesc Rius
1985
This baroque and burlesque park forms an
exception to the generally minimalist trend in
Barcelona's public spaces re-development
programme.

Paret del Valles, main square
Enric Miralles and Carme Pinós
1987
Outside Barcelona, Miralles and Pinós
demonstrated a bold, Constructivist approach.

Parc Creueta del Coll, Barcelona
Josep Mª Martorell, Oriol Bohigas, David Mackay
1981
This park includes a hanging sculpture by Eduardo
Chillida.

El Gambrinus bar, Barcelona
Javier Mariscal and Alfredo Arribas
1988

This bar formed part of Barcelona's waterfront 'opening out to the sea' strategy planned by architect Manuel de Solà-Morales (below). Covering a sunken road, the decks of the Moll de la Fusta allowed pedestrian access from the *chiringuitos* — beach bars — to the waterfront via two bridges. Mariscal's and Arribas's bar was conceived as an epic sea-disaster story, with an immaculate ocean-liner style interior contrasting with a ship wreckage exterior. The surfing, smiling prawn on the roof was intended as a cheeky counterpoint to the 1886 monument to Christopher Columbus situated at the other end of the waterfront.

Mies pavilion, Barcelona
Original 1929 design by Mies van der Rohe
Reconstruction directed by Cristian Cirici, Fernando Solas and Ignasi de Solà-Morales
1986
The rebuilding of Mies's famous pavilion for the 1929 Exhibition symbolically re-established Barcelona as an historical seat of modern proposals in design. Mostly known before restoration through black and white photographs, it was now revealed in all its startling richness and expressiveness.

A/2 clothes shop, Manresa
Pepe Cortés
1987

Above left: Detail of door handle

Above right: Main floor featuring New York armchair
by Nancy Robbins (1987) and the Nordica lamp by
Equipo Santa & Cole (1987).

Opposite: Basement showing excavation which
marks the character of the project, appearing to turn
it into an archaeological dig.

Left: Si-Si-Si bar, Barcelona
Gabriel Ordeig and Carlos Riart
1985
One of the earlier generation of new bars in the Ensanche district, Si-Si-Si clearly demonstrates the tendency towards a 1950s style.

Left and above: Universal bar, Barcelona
Claret Serrahima
1985

Opposite right: Otto Zutz Club, Barcelona
Alícia Nuñez, Jordi Parcerisas, Guillem Bonet
1985

A second wave of bars began to be established in older quarters of Barcelona, using the more irregular and generous spaces of their buildings.

OKB bar, Castelldefels
Gabriel Ordeig
1986
This bar features one of Santa & Cole's most successful products, the Huevo de Colon lamp.

Opposite: Nick Havanna bar, Barcelona, toilets
Eduardo Samsó
1986
Nick Havanna represented a new departure: firstly, in bringing a discothèque proportion and lighting to what remains ostensibly a bar; secondly, in its almost obsessive treatment of details. The design work here began a fresh wave of interest in the toilet facilities of the new bars. Pictogram by Peret.

Above: Nick Havanna bar, Barcelona, main interior
Eduardo Samsó
1986
Stools by Transatlántic to complement the cowhide bar, with chairs by Philippe Starck.

Network Café, Barcelona
Alfredo Arribas and Eduardo Samsó
1986
Network was developed around futuristic images
offered by, for example, the films *Blade Runner* and
Brasil. Within this Postmodern bunker, however,
conviviality is encouraged by the careful use of
objects to provoke social interaction.

Velvet bar, Barcelona
Alfredo Arribas
1987
Velvet was intended as a reaction against the colder
tendencies of Nick Havanna and Network. As such,
it was to invoke something of the atmosphere of the
film *Blue Velvet*.

Louis Vega discothèque, Calafell, Tarragona
Alfredo Arribas
1988
Stretching over 3,000 square metres, this
discothèque complex reflects the increasingly
ambitious plans laid out for night entertainment.
The logo-emblem is by Pati Nuñez and Sonsoles
Llorens.

Capote Club, Madrid
Patrocinio Soriano and Mariano del Olmo
1989
Drawing on images of science fiction from the
1950s as the iconography of optimism, Capote Club
demonstrates that movements in new interior
design were well established outside Barcelona by
the close of the 1980s.

products

Tools for Industrial Reconversion

P RODUCT DESIGN IS PERHAPS THE LEAST developed and most debated design discipline in Spain. It is least developed mostly because of Spain's economic structure. It is a hotly debated issue partly because of the contradictory relationship it has with furniture design. On the one hand, nearly all Spain's product designers are also furniture designers. They are, in effect, industrial designers. The term 'industrial designer', unlike in, for example, Britain, but like in Italy, encompasses both the product and the furniture designer. On the other hand, the inherent differences between each activity cause divisions and almost irresolvable methodological problems within the ranks of industrial designers. Much of the destiny of Spanish design hinges on this debate.

It is not difficult to see why, from the outset, industrial designers tended towards projects in furniture and lighting rather than products. As we have already seen, many of Spain's first industrial designers came to design from architecture, via interior design. Architects such as Martorell-Bohigas-Mackay and Correa-Milà, who worked on small projects such as shops and single houses in the late 1950s and 1960s, found that they also had to design furniture for them.

For the majority of designers of subsequent generations, furniture has been a more satisfactory means of expression for them. Ramón Isern knew that he could work on a piece of furniture, with its relative cheapness in development, while other commissions were not forthcoming. As we have seen in Chapter 2, many designers set up their own furniture editing companies, relying on networks of low-technology workshops to produce the work. Furniture was also a more expressive medium for many designers. Jorge Pensi found furniture more 'metaphorical'. Similarly, it made more sense for Galerias Vinçon to exhibit Bigas Luna's sculptural tables in 1973 than his table calendar, which Disform was producing at the time. Furniture, in other words, carried more cultural

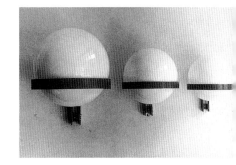

Above: MBM-2 lamp
Martorell-Bohigas-Mackay
Polinax S.A.
1966
This lamp was one of the many fittings designed by the MBM architectural studio which subsequently found wide usage.

Opposite: Arista door handle and lock
Brass
Josep Lluscà
Sellex S.A.
1989

Above: *CAU*, September 1970, monograph dedicated exclusively to industrial design. Designed by Enric Satué.
The years 1968 to 1972 saw a particularly virulent debate over the destiny, meaning and political positions of industrial design in Spanish consumer society.

value than other designed objects. This was as much true in those early heady days of the 1960s and 70s as it was in the design-boom years of the decade that followed.

However, the wider debate about the need to reconcile cultural elitism with the requirements of industry was not satisfactorily resolved. As committed internationalists, designers in Spain were aware of the concerns about design expressed by such colleagues as Victor Papanek, the members of Archigram and Tomás Maldonado of the Ulm school – 1971 was, after all, the year of the ICSID Ibiza conference. Additionally, at home, they lived amidst the material chaos of the so-called economic miracle of Francoism during the *años de desarollo*. Their international awareness and the national context in which they lived meant that reconciling their belief in design with an opposition to the consumer society was doubly difficult. Writing in the architectural and planning magazine *CAU* in 1972, Jaume Lores noted: 'The "made in Catalonia" designers repeatedly cry their desire to *go* to industry, and also repeatedly whisper the identification of Industry–Great Prostitute.' The avant-gardist leanings of designers, and the concentration of their projects in provocative furniture that had a limited commercial strength, did not resolve this problem. Lores continued: 'a decade of design splendour has not allowed the industrial designer to be accepted by industry, and has promoted a very well-organized professional conclusion... Is *Made in Catalonia 1971* design a profession or a cultural movement?.' This confusion, he argued, meant that designers had not fully addressed the issue of working in industry, nor industry been properly able to understand what design entailed. Rather, he saw 'the brief local history of design as being the misfortunes of a cultural movement that has ended up opening a *boutique*'.

By the late 1980s, this problem still had not gone away. In interviews published in *El Món* (1987) and *Design* (1988), the president (Pere Aguirre) and the director (Mai Felip) of the Barcelona Centre of Design both expressed their annoyance with the way designers of furniture had marginalized themselves from industry by concentrating on the more artistic end of projects, and not getting their hands dirty. Unfortunately, and understandably, the exhibitions of the BCD, in particular the itinerant exhibition, *Design in Catalonia*, which began its world tour in Milan in March 1988, was dominated by furniture. This problem did not merely lie with the cultural preferences of designers. It was rare that designers would be absorbed into industry, given Spain's unbalanced industrial structure. This imbalance lay between large industries, which related to the Instituto Nacional de Industria, or were foreign-owned, and an underdeveloped and uncoordinated small-scale industry.

Until the early 1980s, money-losing firms were traditionally placed under the INI umbrella to camouflage national deficits and maintain social peace. Thus, since lame ducks were supported, there was little scope for innovation and thus employment of industrial designers. The only INI exception to this was the unexceptional example of Artespaña, the Madrid-based company formed in the late 1960s to promote Spanish handicraft. It subsequently absorbed designers into its activities, though remained purely in the realm of furnishings. The emphasis was on developing traditional Spanish types, such as an updated eighteenth-century chair by Pedro Miralles, most of which were manufactured, in fact, in the Philippines. Artespaña, in other words, hardly existed as a model company for the promotion of product design in Spain.

Since 1984, as part of government reforms of the economy, INI has moved towards acting as a private company; it even became moderately profitable by the end of the decade. Thirty of its firms were sold off, though this still left it in control of fifty of its large corporations. Among those sold was the Sociedad Española de Autómoviles de Turismo (SEAT), of which the German Volkswagen company bought up a 60 per cent share in 1986, rising to 100 per cent by 1990. For Spanish industrial designers this move represented a worrying shift. SEAT had traditionally made cars under licence from the Italian FIAT. Indeed, the SEAT 600, first brought out in 1957, became – in its small way – as much a symbol of familial mobility and achievement as had its counterpart in Italy (the ideology of which was satirized in Marco Ferreri's 1960 film, *El Cochecito*): between 1957 and 1973, 783,753 were produced. With the breaking of the dependency on FIAT, SEAT had its first opportunity to develop a truly home-grown car. The resulting product was the SEAT Ibiza. Spanish involvement on the design front was, however, limited. The Barcelonese consultancy, Quod, worked on its interior; otherwise, it was a truly international car, with a Porsche engine, components from FIAT and the Ital Design group working on its body styling. Furthermore, the development of subsequent models was undertaken by the continual exchange of proposals between the SEAT design team of ten in Barcelona, and the Volkswagen's four-hundred-strong team in Germany. Under such conditions, it was unlikely that a tradition of high-quality car design would be quickly fostered in Spain.

Many non-INI industries had been foreign dominated, including the British Land Rover works in Seville and the presence of Braun and Olivetti in Barcelona. The last two were admired as models of good design policies, but none the less the designs of Dieter Rams and Ettore Sottsass, who were their respective designers, were rarely matched. As Lores noted in 1972: 'That ineffable television advert, *designed by decorators*, is an example of the undeniable services given by the design movement to the National Industry. But this indirect influence is not the way to arrive at an *Olivetti & Braun and Sons, Ltd...* It's only the means by which the plagiarists need not make so many foreign journeys, and

Above: SEAT Ibiza
First launched in 1984, the SEAT Ibiza was subsequently marketed as the ideal 'Euro-car' rather than something specifically Spanish.

the manufacturer … makes a trip to peruse the design *boutiques*, with – or without – the pretext of buying a wedding present.'

As foreign investment in Spain increased substantially in the late 1980s – between 1985 and 1987 it rose from 280,085 million pesetas to 727,279 million pesetas – the problem of creating a specific identity in Spanish product design became more immediate. Crys of 'Se vende el país' (country for sale) were heard among the more frustrated Spaniards, who saw the opportunity to consolidate a national design identity being swamped by rapid internationalization.

Set against the weight of large industries, either foreign controlled or INI administered, few small industries had undertaken product innovation. The protection of industry during the Francoist period meant also that the small industries did not have to compete with foreign competition. While the core industries were unlikely to change, the peripheral small industries were threatened by over dependency on their larger cousins. As suggested in Chapter 2, in the realm of furniture production, the use of small workshop networks certainly pushed up the technical standards attained by them, but it was rare that the result was development of more sophisticated products. One of the few companies to edit products away from furniture and lighting was Miscel.lània de Mercè Bohigas in Barcelona. Founded in 1974 by the husband-and-wife team of Martí Gascon and Mercè Bohigas, Miscel.lània followed in the line set by Disform in editing furnishings; however, unlike Disform, Miscel.lània did not turn to single-piece furniture, but instead developed simple, but innovatory products designed for and directed to an export market. In editing just a few products, such as the Espiral hanger – which first appeared in 1970 and is now even made in Italy under licence from Miscel.lània – and the brilliant Pinça-Plus shelving bracket – the world's only bracket developed to clasp rather than support the shelf – they were able to produce and export in small batches.

It was in a context in which designers and manufacturers were closely connected that product design in Spain flourished – Martí Gascon himself was actively connected with ADIFAD and indeed in 1982 formed a shortlived forerunner of SIDI. Through close relationships with members of ADIFAD, a few other manufacturers also provided exceptional examples of product design from the 1960s; these included the domestic electrical equipment manufacturers, Soler i Palau; the plastics company, Aiscondel; the audio-visual goods company, Vieta. In packaging and product presentation, the perfume company, Puig, was particularly important. So disparate are these, however, that one cannot say that an identifiable design type or approach was developed through them over the years. Rather, the development of a *Spanish* product design identity may come through its successive generations of designers.

Above: Extractor fan
Internal team
Soler i Palau S.A.
1965
Founded in 1959, Soler i Palau is one of the few companies that maintained a consistent policy in recognizing international technical and safety standards from its foundation.

Of the first generation, one cannot ignore the figures of André Ricard and Miguel Milà. Having started in product design in the 1950s, both carried a particularly Modernist (and, moreover, anti-Postmodernist) approach through to the 1990s. André Ricard consistently demonstrated in his design work a control and sometimes austere precision in a succession of 'humble objects', as he called them, ranging from his Copenhagen ashtrays for Flamagas, to dinner plates for Bidasoa Porcelana, and coffee machines for Gaggia. Of these the Copenhagen ashtrays are particularly noteworthy from the point of view of material: Spain was remarkably devoid of 'gadgets' or simple plastic items – the Copenhagen ashtray was manufactured from 1966 into the 1990s. As a prolific essayist, commentator and broadcaster, André Ricard also continued a crusade against the possible trivialization of design brought about by its *boom* – his books, *Diseño ¿Por qué?* (1982), *Diseño y calidad de vida* (1985) and *Hablando de Diseño* (1986), all acted as his contributions to a need felt by many Spanish designers in the 1980s: to revivify the strong debates that had existed around design in the late 1960s and early 1970s, as well as to counteract via reflection misplaced design euphoria of the 1980s. In this way, Ricard presented a sober, considered face of design to confused manufacturers considering its application within their company development in the 1990s, but not entirely sure what it all signified; and, in addition, his position acted as a point of reference both for future designers and for the interpretation of their work. Miguel Milà, for his part, demonstrated a steady adherence to 'Good Design' in his successive lighting projects with Polinax, his staircasing for DAE (Diseño Ahorro Energetico) and his brilliant redesign of Barcelona's metro train interiors.

Students who came out of Barcelona's design colleges in the late 1960s invariably turned their hands to product design as they would to any other design discipline – that is, with an intellectual and conceptual dexterity, but not necessarily with a strong technical background. The results were diverse. Ramón Benedito, Gabriel Teixido, Josep Lluscà; Gemma Bernal and Ramón Isern were all involved in projects in product design as well as furniture from the 1970s.

Josep Lluscà's work with Fagor in developing a pressure cooker clearly demonstrates his personal enthusiasm for experimenting with mechanisms. One might venture to say that this activity presents a microcosm of the trajectory of Fagor itself: based in Mondragón in the Basque Country, it was initially unable to attract capital to set itself up – the regional nationalist struggles were not conducive to high investment from outside, and it was set up as a cooperative to manufacture domestic electrical items. As it developed, however, it acquired new skills. Thus when it required a new building, for instance, it developed its own architectural studio building unit; when a new tooling system was required, it developed its own; and so on. In this way, by the end of the 1980s Fagor had

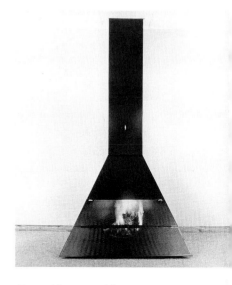

Above: Ximenea chimney
Miguel Milà
Diseño Ahorro Energetico S.A.
Designed 1977

not only maintained its cooperative status – and, indeed, Mondragón itself was the seat of a whole network of hi-tech cooperatively run industries – but was now Spain's leading company in consultation and implementation of tooling systems, as well as manufacturing products from fridges to bicycles. Like Josep Lluscà himself, Fagor's work developed through a combination of innovations and improvisations.

Another notable designer who was closely involved in the industrial developments of Mondragón was Guillermo Capdevila. A graduate of London's Royal College of Art in 1975, with a degree in mechanical engineering obtained before that, he is representative of the Basque tendency towards engineering design. This stems firstly from Bilbao's strong tradition in heavy industries, and secondly, perhaps, from a propensity to send at least some of its students with scholarships to Britain rather than to Italy to study. In combining his engineering background, and therefore strengths in product innovation, with a sharp marketing team, his large consultancy, Capdevila Associates, was very much an exception in Spain. The many much smaller studios tended not to concern themselves with the internal workings of products as much as with the outer shell; nor did they focus on marketing aspects in product development.

In terms of marketing, another exception was Barcelona's Quod. Formed in 1983 by industrial designer Esteve Agulló, architect Mariano Pi, graphic designer Josep Mª Trias and marketing specialist Jordi Montaña, for a while it held a virtual monopoly on large redesign jobs in the Catalan region. A team of over 30 worked on diverse projects, ranging from diagnostic research for Johnny Walker Whisky to furniture for Artespaña. As large design commissions became increasingly internationalized, Quod, with its unusual strengths in size and marketing, was open to and ready for ventures outside Catalonia, perhaps in the direction of joint, multi-national ventures with other consultancies, thereby avoiding the possibility of being swallowed up by foreign competition in Spain.

The most remarkable rise of a large, multi-disciplinary design company in the 1980s must be attributed to Barcelona's Associate Designers. In the space of three years, its directors, industrial designer Ramón Bigas and engineer Pep Sant, energetically steered AD to becoming, by 1990, Spain's biggest design group, with over 50 professionals. Unlike Capdevila Associates and Quod, AD barely concerned itself with marketing, believing instead in the strength of its own products. These included highly successful lamps for Italy's Luxo and America's Zelco, as well as a taxi-metre which superseded Quod's own. Working on a national level, it was also most effective in exhibition stands and pavilions, carrying the advantage against outside competition of having its own implementation team, which was able to see such projects through with greater ease.

Associate Designers' most spectacular job, though, was its work on the Spanish railway network, RENFE. This included redesigning the carriages of both the local and inter-city trains, their interiors, signing and furnishing. The crowning glory of the project was their design work on the high-speed train which was to run from Madrid to Seville, linking the capital to the Expo '92 site. Here, with the collaboration of the avant-garde Catalan poet, Joan Brossa, the train was envisaged as an 'object poem', with the letters of the word *tren* broadly marked across its carriages. The artists Antoni Tàpies and Eduardo Chilida were also involved on the project, but the exciting potential was not to be realized. The British design group, Addison, was brought in by RENFE. Addison's strength in marketing and management secured their visually less adventurous solution. As in graphic design, in the large projects in product and transport design, indigenous design companies offering distinctive approaches were vulnerable to foreign competition. While the foreigners could not necessarily dominate in purely design terms, they often carried superior weight in the realms of marketing and product management. As Pep Sant once remarked to the author: 'In 1492 the Spaniards sailed off and discovered the Indians. Five hundred years later, the discoverers are being discovered and have become the Indians.'

Associate Designers expanded rapidly in response to the complexities of the larger and larger projects they handled. Paradoxically, if more such companies existed in Spain, more work would be secured for them rather than farmed out to foreign companies, since the commissioning organizations would focus on the indigenous skills available. As it is, much of the design work for the Seville Expo '92, for instance, which could have been handled by design groups within Spain, has gone abroad, thus curtailing longer-term developments in the area. Clearly, as we have seen with SEAT, the movement of substantial foreign companies into Spain in the late 1980s is also curtailing opportunities for developments in product design in the realm of large-scale production.

With the exception of large design consultancies, therefore, it may be that product design will develop in the context of smaller studios responding to small and middle-sized producers. The engineering design studio Via Design in Barcelona, with a team of six under the guidance of Joan Suñol, developed many innovatory products with the smaller plastics manufacturers, such as Plásticos Trilla and Plásticos Tatay, in the late 1980s. Even Via Design, which was virtually the only studio involved in both the interior workings and the exterior face of sophisticated products in Catalonia, went through low patches. Ripples in the Spanish economy, such as a slowing down of credit in late 1989, paralysed the growth of smaller industries, and thus their willingness to invest in design.

In Valencia, two studios emerged in the 1980s which suggested a positive route forward in product design. One is Factoria Diseño Industrial. All four core

Above: Regulating and stabilizing
voltage supply systems
Factoria Diseño Industrial
A.B.C. Electronica
1989

members studied with IMPIVA (Institut de la Mitjana i Petita Indústria Valen-ciana), and had grants at either the Scuola Politecnica di Design or the Istituto Europeo de Design in Milan, before setting up Factoria Diseño Industrial in early 1987. Their stay in Milan of 1984-85 had primarily influenced them in a Memphis direction: 'Many preoccupations with expression, without rigorously considering the construction and working of the object,' they later declared. Subsequently, they aimed more towards working in product design than in furniture, acknowledging the influence of the Milan-based designers Santiago Miranda and Perry King in their application of a conceptual agility to product design, but also displaying a reading of more everyday objects, and a response to Rationalist design of the 1950s. Thus they set about transferring an Italianate experience of design to their own interpretation of history and surroundings.

Members of La Nave (already introduced in Chapter 3), whilst not directly benefiting from a Milanese design education, brought a fresh, youthful flavour to product design which was already evident in their graphic work. This touched projects that included Marisa Gallén and Sandra Figuerola's playful, if not ludicrous inflatables, through to Daniel Nebot and Nacho Lavernia's roof-rack system or their coded public fountain.

By the 1990s, it was clear that in packaging, corporate identity and product design for massive production, a national design identity – perhaps developing through furniture, interior design and public spaces – had given way to the inevitable Pan-Europeanism of multi-nationals. Despite a slowing up of the economic growth of Spain in the early 1990s, new alliances and organizations in industry – at the level of small and middle-sized companies – would be formed, which in turn would create new opportunities for innovation. Industry, in short, would be more geared up to participate on the European circuit, offering goods which would be of Spanish identity rather than 'typical Spanish'. At the level of smaller studios serving local industries, new strengths, as demonstrated by La Nave, were beginning to emerge. This had the extra effect of to some extent distributing the focus of design activity away from Barcelona, thus ensuring that new Spanish design would become a more Spanish-wide, but also regional affair. As such it would maintain its diversity, but also its energy. At the same time, there would be a consolidation of quality, meaning relatively fewer desig-ners, but more Design as a tool for industrial reconversion.

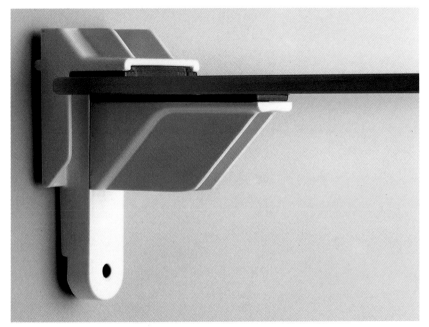

Left, top and centre: Pinca Plus shelving bracket
Injected aluminium
Mariano Ferrer
Miscel.lània de Mercè Bohigas
1986
By clasping instead of supporting shelving this bracket can be used for any kind of shelf (marble, glass, etc.) Its original design has been a protagonist for Miscel.lània, one of the few Spanish companies that edits products rather than furniture.

Left: Fond ashtrays
Ramón Benedito
Miscel.lània de Mercé Bohigas
1989

Above: B.D. extractor fan
Oscar Tusquets, Lluís Clotet and Anna Bohigas
B.D. Ediciones de Diseño
1979
As well as furniture, fittings and rugs, B.D. also edits innovatory products. This hood is transparent so that the user may lower it and still see to cook.

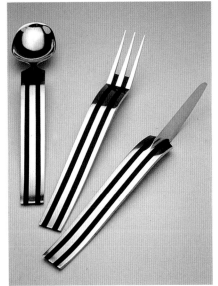

Top left: Oceano sink
Sangres S.A.L.
1987

Far left: Cutlery designed in the late 1960s.

Left: Pongotodo waste-bin
Plásticos Tatay S.A.
1983

Top right: Porcelain dinner set
Porcelanas del Bidasoa S.A.
1988

Above: Fichet alarm
Fichet S.A.
1989

Spain's pioneering product designer, André Ricard, has worked on a wide variety of projects, though always with a clear Modernist tendency.

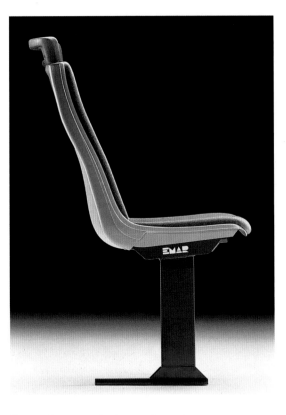

Above: Nova seat for bus and coach
Quod Diseño y Marketing
Emar S.A.
1988/9

Above right: Blue Fox electric toy car
Quod Diseño y Marketing
Feber S.A.
1986

One of Spain's few multi-disciplinary large design
companies, Quod Diseño y Marketing is also
virtually unique in its marketing-led design
management.

Right: Splendid pressure cooker
Josep Lluscà
Fagor S.C.
1986
A combination of a broad training with an openness
to different challenges has resulted in many
designers such as Lluscà working in a wide variety of
design disciplines, including more technical
product design.

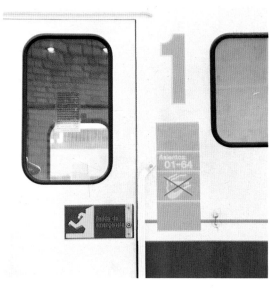

Top left: Cabin for high-speed locomotive
(Locomotora Alta Velocidad 269-600) for RENFE
1989

Above: Graphics for exterior of Inter-City train for
RENFE
1988

Opposite: Inter-City Electrotren exterior for RENFE
1988

Opposite, inset: Interior of commuter train Cercanía
446 for RENFE
1988

Far left: Altalena halogen desk lamp
Luxo, Italy
1985

Centre left: Packaging for Altalena lamp

Bottom left: Exhibition stand. Tecnoalimentaria '89
1989

With a strong engineering background, but with
virtually no marketing, Associate Designers grew in
the late 1980s to be one of Spain's most potent
design companies, their work ranging from
extensive re-designing of the country's railway
system to exhibition stands, including much work
for the Seville Expo '92. Apart from their rarity as a
large engineering design company, one of their
greatest assets (particularly over foreign
competition) was knowing the local ground.

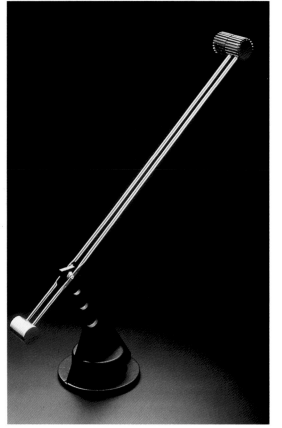

Left: Roof racks
Daniel Nebot and Nacho Lavernia, La Nave
Indústrias Saludes S.A.
1986

Above: Water fountain
Daniel Nebot and Nacho Lavernia, La Nave
Indústrias Saludes S.A.
1986

Above: Sation 1000 syphon
Joan Suñol—Via Design
Sation S.A.
1988

Above right: Multiband amplifier
Joan Suñol—Via Design
Tedel S.A.
1989

Right: Sprayer
Jaume Edo—Via Design
Channel S.A.
1988

Both La Nave in Valencia and Via Design in
Barcelona offer engineering design for small- and
medium-sized manufacturing companies. If, by the
end of the 1980s, companies in this sector were
sometimes slow on the uptake in re-organizing
themselves, and also suffering from unfavourable
government fiscal policy with high interest rates
putting a brake on investment, some achievements
did suggest new strengths in Spanish product
design into the 1990s.

Above left: Tableware
Andres Nagel
Porcelanas del Bidasoa S.A.
1988

Above right: Florero jar
Javier Mariscal
Porcelanas del Bidasoa S.A.
1988

With a rich tradition in ceramics, and as Europe's
second exporter of them, Spain was bound to make
efforts to modify the industry, seen particularly in
the Valencia region. In the meantime, however, the
Basque company, Porcelanas del Bidasoa, had a
long history of using designers and artists such as
André Ricard, Salvador Dalí and Raymond Loewy.

chronology

1888   Universal Exhibition in Barcelona.

1903   Hispano Suiza launch the first car manufactured in Spain.
Fomento de las Artes Decorativas (FAD) founded in Barcelona.

1923   Military coup of General Primo de Rivera.

1929   International Exhibition in Barcelona: Mies van der Rohe constructs the German pavilion.

1930   Creation of GATEPAC in Zaragoza and GATCPAC in Barcelona.

1931   Second Republic proclaimed on 14 April.

1931–36   Period of development of Rationalism in design and architecture.

1936   Civil War begins on 17–18 July.

1939   Civil War ends on 1 April and the Francoist dictatorship is established.

1951   Grup R founded in Barcelona. Henceforth, a recuperation of Rationalism and its debate.

1957   Attempt to form the Instituto de Diseño Industrial de Barcelona (IDIB) with the support of Gio Ponti.
Franco forms sixth government, including technocrats of the Opus Dei, signalling end of the Autarchy and beginnings of the *años de desarollo* (development years).

1959   The Escuela Massana (school of arts and crafts) in Barcelona begins courses in graphic design.
Foundation of FAD school.

1960   Agrupación de Diseño Industrial del Fomento de las Artes Decorativas (ADIFAD) founded.

1961   ADIFAD joins the International Council for Societies of Industrial Design (ICSID).

1961   Agrupación de Diseño Gráfico del FAD (ADGFAD) founded.
Foundation of Elisava design school.

1965   Student anti-Francoist agitation stepped up in Madrid and Barcelona. Department of Industrial Design formed at the Escuela Massana.

1966   Schism within Elisava leads to foundation of Eina experimental school of art and design.

1967   Gruppo 63 seminar takes place at Eina, with Gillo Dorfles and Umberto Eco, among many others.

1968   Spain's Massiel wins the Eurovision Song Contest with 'La, La, La'.

1971   ICSID conference held in Ibiza, organized by ADIFAD.

1973   Foundation of Barcelona Centre de Disseny, with the objectives of the promotion, investigation and information of design in Spain.
La Sala Vinçon puts on first exhibition with Bigas Luna's 'Taules'.

1975   Franco dies on 20 November.

1977 Partial autonomy for Catalonia with re-opening of the Generalitat. Abolition of the National Movement, the political base of the Franco regime. First general elections since 1936 held on 15 June, the victor the centrist Unión Centro Democrático.

1978 EEC approves Spanish application on 29 November.
Spain's first design magazine, *On*, founded.
Asociación de Diseñadores Profesionales (ADP) formed.

1979 General election on 1 March. UCD retain power.

1980 Oriol Bohigas becomes delegate of l'Area d'Urbanisme of the Barcelona City Council (succeeded by Josep Acebillo), which instigates urban renovation programme.

Oscar Tusquets is invited to take part in Alessi's Tea or Coffee Set project.

1981 Picasso's *Guernica* returns to Spain from New York.
Zig-Zag bar by Alícia Nuñez and Guillem Bonet begins new wave of bar interiors in Barcelona.
Javier Mariscal collaborates with the Memphis group in Milan.

1982 General Election on 18 October. Partido Socialista Obrero Español under Felipe González wins and retains power for the rest of the 1980s.

1983 Salón Internacional de Diseño del Equipamiento para el Habitat (SIDI) formed.

1984 Institut de la Mitjana i Petita Indústria Valenciana (IMPIVA) formed in Valencia, incorporating design section.

Industri Diseinurako Zentrua (DZ) founded in Bilbao.

1985 ADIFAD, ADGFAD, ADP and BCD organize 'Diseño España – Europalia '85' in Brussels, Spain's first major exhibition of design.

1986 Spanish accession to the EEC.
Mies van der Rohe's 1929 Barcelona pavilion reconstructed.
Nick Havanna bar, by Eduardo Samsó, opened in Barcelona.
SIDI stands achieve major success and recognition at the Milan Furniture Fair.

1992 Single European Market.
Barcelona hosts Olympic Games.
Seville hosts World Expo.
Madrid is Cultural Capital of Europe.
500th anniversary of Christopher Columbus's discovery of America.

biographies: designers, companies, studios

Fernando Amat (b. 1941)

It is no exaggeration to say that in Spanish design nearly all routes pass Fernando Amat's door. The particular door in question is his shop Vinçon, situated in Barcelona next to Gaudí's La Pedrera (otherwise known as the Casa Milà), where he lives. Since 1967, Vinçon has been unique in that it is a large shop offering to the public a wide range of quality household objects – a philosophy based somewhat on Terence Conran's Habitat stores. However, beyond this, Amat has been highly influential in encouraging designers, design companies and even other retailers. Vinçon's own exhibition room, La Sala Vinçon, has been an important platform for exposing both national and international design work. In addition to running Vinçon, Fernando Amat has produced two films (*Tatuaje* and *Bilbao*) with Bigas Luna, owned a restaurant, La Venta, and even designed a bar, Merbeye, with Mariscal in 1978. Without any philosophy of design, he may just as easily put on display a fan from India or an imitation log fire from England as the latest piece of Barcelona design.

Barcelona Centre de Disseny (f. 1973)

Following the euphoria of the 1971 ICSID conference in Ibiza, organized by ADIFAD, and the success of FAD's stand at the Hogarotel trade fair of the same year, CODI (Consejeros de Diseño) was formed by the industrial designer, Joan Antoni Blanc, with the aim of creating a design centre. This soon turned into the Barcelona Centre de Disseny, destined to raise the public profile of design and promote design in industry. Interestingly, the previous year Blanc had left the staff of Eina, protesting at its neglect of product design studies in favour of more culturalist design pursuits found in interior and furniture design. This move represented a schism felt generally among many industrial designers, and in some respects marked the character of the Barcelona Centre de Disseny for years to come. Unlike many design centres in other countries, the BCD, however, was a foundation without any direct aid from the administration. Initially, support came from Jordi Pujol, who was then director of the Banca Catalana and influential in the Barcelona Chamber of Commerce, with resulting financial aid from savings banks, institutions and friends of the city. Sufficient funding was therefore available for both cultural and commercial activities. By the end of the 1970s, both these aspects were severely curtailed when, through pressure from the economic crisis, sponsorship was withdrawn. The centre's reconstruction in the 1980s was much more directed towards economic development and the industrial reconversion of Catalonia, in particular by the establishment of a design audit system, linking industry with designers. Such projects were now funded by the Catalan regional government, the Generalitat, as was its itinerant exhibition, 'Design in Catalonia', which first opened in Milan in 1987 and has travelled to Osaka and New York, among other cities.

While the BCD does hold considerable historical importance in the promotion of design within Spain, special mention should also be made of Bilbao's Industri Diseinurako Zentrua (DZ) and Valencia's Institut de la Mitjana i Petita Indústria Valenciana (IMPIVA), both formed in 1984. DZ was set up by a Basque administrative body, the Diputación Foral de Bizkaia, and acts exclusively in the promotion of industrial design, with similar activities to the BCD. IMPIVA comes under the Conselleria d'Indústria, Comerç i Turisme, of the Generalitat Valenciana. As such, its design section forms an integral part of the region's global economic development policy.

Oriol Bohigas (1925)

No account of the development of Spanish design is complete without the inclusion of Oriol Bohigas; while his personal activity has been primarily as an architect, he has had great influence on the character of Spanish design. Having qualified as an architect at the Escuela de Arquitectura de Barcelona in 1951, Bohigas has worked with Josep Martorell ever since, incorporating David Mackay into his studio from 1961 to form MBM, and later being joined by Lluís Pau (1974). He was a founder-member of Grup R (1951–58), important for its revindication of the Modernist proposals of the GATCPAC group of the 1930s during a period otherwise marked by architectural conservatism. By the early 1960s, he was a leader of the Realist architecture movement in Catalonia, combining Modernist principles with local vernacular methods of construction. In the modification of doctrines and styles, he thus laid the theoretical ground for generations to come. The individualistic scale of projects and sense of detail (often involving interior and some product design), as well as the interest in history without pastiche, were also influential features of his theory and practice. His publications include *Barcelona entre el Pla Cerdà i el barraquisme* (1963), *Arquitectura modernista* (1963), *Contra una arquitectura adjetivada* (1969), *Polèmica d'arquitectura catalana* (1970) and *Reconstrucció de Barcelona* (1985). From 1964 to 1966 he was a lecturer at the Escuela de Arquitectura de Barcelona; however, like his colleague Frederico Correa, he had a stormy political relationship with the university authorities. Their marginalization from the Escuela de Arquitectura meant that their attentions were turned to the benefit of the private design schools, in particular to Eina. In

1970 he regained his position at the Escuela de Arquitectura, but was sacked within months, the course he planned to teach being translated into a publication, *Proceso y erótica del diseño* (1972). As a leading spokesman of the shortlived Escuela de Barcelona (approximately 1968–71), he crystallized such ideas, which also included the importance of the use of, and sometimes ironic play on, visual languages in design, which in its turn may be interpreted as a Postmodern position. On the other hand, he has also faithfully adhered to some Modernist principles, particularly in raising the importance of urban planning as the hub of architectural activity. In this respect, his appointment as representative of l'Area d'Urbanisme to the new Barcelona City Council in 1980 (succeeded by Josep Acebillo in 1984) ensured the urban revitalization of the city. This was achieved, typically, by urban design rather than town planning, meaning the concentration on the renewal of parks and plazas, instead of a wholesale restructuring of areas. This approach has had important resonances for the conception of town planning in other countries; more specifically, it has brought a concept of design closer to the everyday lives of Catalan and Spanish citizens.

Juli Capella (b. 1960) and Quim Larrea (b. 1958)

Since training as architects, Capella and Larrea have become Spain's leading *animateurs* of new design. In 1983–84 they coordinated ten editions of Spain's first design magazine, *On*, then in the same year became founder directors of *De Diseño*, a design magazine that emerged from the Madrid-based architectural magazine, *El Croquis*. Seeking a more internationally orientated publication, in 1988 they founded *Ardi*, which they have directed ever since.

Additionally, they broadcast, appear on many 'design juries' and organize exhibitions. Their energetic activities lend credence to the thought that the development of design in Spain is closely bound to the development of its debate and consciousness through its literature.

Alexandre Cirici (1914–1983)

Although primarily an art critic and historian, Alexandre Cirici played an important role in the development of modern design in Spain during its early years. Two of his most notable qualities were the broadness of his interests and his radical politics. Thus, his famous article 'L'art de la saviesa' in the Catalan magazine *Ariel* (1946) championed Catalan artists and writers alongside others of the international Modern Movement, but ends with the assertion that one should take interest in the everyday object, implicitly setting this against the gestural rhetoric of Francoism. In 1955 he undertook a *licenciatura* thesis on the history of industrial design at the University of Barcelona – a radical and unusual step for its time – which he published in a summarized form in the clandestine magazine *Quart Creixant*. Cirici was at the centre of the foundation of the FAD school of design in Barcelona in 1959 and ADIFAD in 1960, and subsequently Elisava in 1961 and Eina in 1966. Being at the heart of the formulation of each school's methodologies, he was influential in establishing their strong conceptual and reflective components. Through his own writing (especially in the Catalan magazine *Serra d'Or* during the 1960s and 1970s) and the activities of the different design schools, one may clearly trace the development of design teaching away from a Bauhaus- or Ulm School-inspired methodology to a reading based more in structuralism and semiotics. Albert

Ràfols Casamada wrote of Cirici: 'His basic idea was that a school shouldn't give a repertoire of solutions to standard problems, but it should teach proper ways to consider problems. Thus the teaching of design became eminently conceptual.' Two ex-students of his, Alicia Suárez and Merce Vidal, wrote: 'He informed us about thinkers of diverse areas and disciplines and amplified our conception of things with a sharp critique of established values.' Two years before his death in 1983, he became a deputy in the Council of Europe.

Quim Larrea see Juli Capella

Alberto Liévore (b.1948) and Jorge Pensi (b.1949)

Liévore and Pensi studied architecture in Buenos Aires, later establishing themselves in Barcelona in 1977. As Pensi once said: 'With a training in architecture, I can design anything from a screw to a building.' Thus, their projects have been multi-various, including the SIDI stands and much of the Latina range of the furniture company, Perobell (as well as its graphics work). With Oriol Pibernat and Norberto Chaves, they formed the design consultancy Grupo Berenguer. However, from 1984 they have increasingly worked separately, although both highly rate the investigative and communicative elements of design. Pensi's Toledo chair (1988) developed aluminium casting for furniture while at the same time reinventing the language of outdoor furniture. Liévore's attentions have been turned to the reworking of traditional typologies in furniture, such as in the Manolete (1988), whilst also investigating more product-design related problems.

Josep Lluscà (b.1948)

A prodigy of the first student intake of the Escola Eina, Josep Lluscà learnt very early on that one's conceptual dexterity came first, and the technical aspects of design later. As with many young designers, economic necessity caused him to work in a wide range of design disciplines during the 1970s. While he produced many splendid pieces of product design in the 1980s, as the decade progressed he concentrated more exclusively on furniture and lighting. Likening his approach to that of a sculptor, he none the less considers both the expressive and ergonomic aspects of design with scientific rigour. In order to achieve these values, his researches may range widely, sometimes incorporating both Gaudí and 1950s Rationalistic elements into the same piece.

Javier Mariscal (b.1950)

Though born in Valencia, from the early 1970s he was more closely associated with the 'underground' comics that circulated around Barcelona's Plaça Real. Despite his lack of formal training, his sketchy and irreverent style of comic drawing found its way by chance to be applied to various design projects in the 1980s. Via design work on a bar with Fernando Salas in Valencia in 1980 and subsequently an exhibition of *Muebles Amorales* (amoral furniture) at the Sala Vinçon with Pepe Cortes in the same year, Mariscal came to the attention of Ettore Sottsass, who invited him to take part in the Memphis show of 1981. Thus he shot to international fame and since has been in high demand, applying his skills to projects ranging from sofas, to textile designs, to the Olympic mascot for 1992.

Miguel Milà (b.1931)

One of the first generation of industrial designers in Spain. After an unsatisfying education at the Escuela de Arquitectura de Barcelona, Milà moved into design, working with his archirect brother, Alfonso Milà, and with Frederico Correa. Among his first and most well-known designs is the TMC lamp, first conceived in 1956 and manufactured by various producers (including himself) with subsequent modifications ever since. Bridging the influence of J.A. Coderch and the Grup R of the 1950s to the present, this lamp has become something of a classic and a cult symbol of the survival of modern proposals in design through this period. After receiving the National Design Prize in 1987, Milà found it difficult to reconcile his Modernistic leanings with the colour of 1980s designerly hype. He has recently returned to designing, aware of the new possibilities that the reorganization of industry allows.

Pedro Miralles (b.1955)

Born in Valencia, and finishing architectural studies in Madrid in 1980, Miralles has become one of the major presences amongst new Spanish designers. He undertook a Masters at the Domus Academy in Milan in 1987, an experience which is sometimes reflected in his quirky, poetic furniture designs. At the same time, he has also benefitted from the literary and artistic atmosphere of Madrid within which he moves – indeed, his work includes collaborations with film-maker Pedro Almodovar.

La Nave (f.1984)

Lacking the cultural and economic traditions of Barcelona, Valencia has had to go further in less time in order to build a design identity. However, with a strong industrial base in the manufacture of furniture, ceramics and toys, Valencia during the 1980s gradually nurtured a design capacity that grew *through* industry rather than *in spite of* it. Two studios, Caps i Mans and Enebecé found an increasing coincidence in clients and projects, and thus merged to form La Nave, offering multi-disciplinary design services. Its eleven core members came from a variety of backgrounds, from fine art, in the cases of Sandra Figuerola, Marisa Gallén and Luis González, graphic design in the case of Paco Bascuñán and Lorenzo Company, or architecture in the case of Carlos Bento. La Nave's activities have not been bridled by any design philosophy or approach, and this has allowed freshness and originality into their projects, making them a potent force in Spanish design for the 1990s.

Jorge Pensi see Alberto Liévore

Peret (b.1945)
Born as Pere Torrent, he began his career as an illustrator and graphic designer for different advertising agencies and publishing firms in 1965. In 1970 he moved to Paris, where he became art director of Prisunic and Delpire-Advico before working freelance with, amongst others, *Marie-Claire*, Air France and Citroën. He returned to Barcelona in 1978. Much of his graphic style derives from studies of movements in fine art, taking in Constructivism, Cubism through to Figurative Expressionism; at the same time, some of his illustrations include provocative, or even explicit features. Known in Barcelona mostly through his posters for the city council's cultural events, and for his illustrations for the newspaper *La Vanguardia*, his work also extends to the video graphics company Anamática and to wine labels.

Carlos Riart (b.1944)
Having undertaken an apprenticeship as a cabinet maker, but also being one of Eina's first students, Riart has moved between traditional craft activity and the avant-garde. His long association with Bigas Luna led them to set up Gris in 1968, a pioneer in interior design shops in Barcelona. His important exhibition, 'Primera Colección de Muebles' (1976) was of highly finished cabinet work, which, however, broke from traditional furniture typologies. It has often been described as 'Memphis before Memphis'. Ever since, he has continued this approach of 'innovating within a tradition', producing work for Knoll International, Disform and, most recently, working exclusively within Muebles Casas.

André Ricard (b.1929)
Sent to London to learn English in the early 1950s, he became involved in design work at the time of the Festival of Britain. On returning to Spain, he began to design 'humble objects' in his family pharmaceutical supply firm, though still not fully aware of such a concept as industrial design. It was through contact with the growing theoretical literature on industrial design, in particular that of Raymond Loewy (whom he first met in 1956), that he formed a clearer picture of the role of the industrial designer. Subsequently, apart from being Spain's pioneering product designer, he was also a prolific writer, publishing three books, *Diseño ¿Por qué?* (1982), *Diseño y calidad de vida* (1985) and *Hablando de diseño* (1987). He was Vice-President of the International Council for Societies of Industrial Design (ICSID) (1963–67 and 1976–79) and organizer of its 'Design for Rescue and Relief' project in the 1970s. He was also the force behind the foundation of the Agrupación de Diseño Industrial del Fomento de las Artes Decorativas (ADIFAD) in 1960. He

was thus highly important in the consolidation of Spanish design at an institutional and theoretical level. His product design (for Moulinex, Metalarte, Gaggia, among many others) demonstrates a clear Modernist tendency, and he has been an open critic of the excesses of Postmodernism. None the less, his packaging design (particularly work for perfume companies such as Puig and Paco Rabanne) demonstrates a keen awareness of the communicative over the functionalist aspects of design, a direction in which he has moved in recent years.

Salón Internacional de Diseño del Equipamiento para el Habitat (SIDI) (f.1983)
Born out of Spain's first design magazine, *On* (f.1978), under the direction of Carme Ferrer and Carme Llopis, SIDI grew as a response to the problem of the commercialization of Spanish design products. It thus established itself as an umbrella organization for companies manufacturing and editing furnishings, in turn providing a platform for their stands at furniture fairs. From its first appearance at the Valencia Furniture Fair in 1984, SIDI consolidated the image of Spanish designer products in the international market via representations in nearly all the major European furniture fairs. While SIDI exists as an organization open to all comers, its designerly leanings mean that it does not account for the entire sector of furniture in Spain. None the less, between 1983 and 1988, its members' exports grew by 449 per cent, with the USA and France heading the lists of buyers.

Enric Satué (b.1938)
Both as a designer and promoter of graphic design, Enric Satué occupies an important position in the consolidation of graphics in

Spain. After experiences in advertising agencies, he was to open out his design in 1970 when he began work on the rupturist architectural magazine, *CAU*, which was to reach a public beyond architects and introduce the concept of modern graphic design in Barcelona. The graphics he employed were informed by his knowledge of international movements in graphics (particularly Milton Glaser and Roman Cieslewicz). At the same time, however, in their subversive irony and play on images, they fell within the attitudes current in other design disciplines at the time. While the visual results of his various projects may be very different, the suggestion that the image may have several sets of readings runs through his work. In parallel with his design work, Satué has written extensively on graphic design, including an exhaustive world history of graphic design, *El diseño gráfico: Desde los origenes hasta nuestros días* (1988). Through exhibitions and publications, he has recovered much of Spain's lost history of graphic design.

Oscar Tusquets (b.1941)

A graduate of the Escuela de Arquitectura de Barcelona in 1965, Tusquets formed Studio Per with his classmates Lluís Clotet, Cristian Cirici and Pep Bonet. Having previously worked in the architectural studio of Correa-Milà, Tusquets was well connected with avant-garde architects in Barcelona who would later make up the loose alliance of architects known as the Escuela de Barcelona. He has often been seen as Spain's representative of Postmodernism, mostly following his Belvedere de Regàs (1972). This is a label he himself would now reject as too orthodox a concept. His activities are multi-various, ranging from painting, through interior and product design, to architecture. Likewise, the styles he adopts are eclectic, ranging through Pop, Modernista, Conceptual and neo-Classical influences. As such, he might only suit the widest possible definition of Postmodernism. In 1973, Studio Per and others, in particular Xavier Carulla, formed B.D. Ediciones de Diseño, to produce designs which no one else would risk manufacturing at the time.

design on show: galleries, museums, shops

France

Edifice
27 bis, Bd. Raspail
Paris

Nestor Perkal
8 rue des Quatre Fils
Paris

Spain

Adelantado Muebles
Paz, 33
Valencia

B.D. Ediciones de Diseño
Mallorca, 291
Barcelona

B.D. Ediciones de Diseño
Villanueva, 5
Madrid

Pilma
Diagonal 403
Barcelona

Vinçon
Paseo de Gracia, 96
Barcelona

UK

The Conran Shop
Michelin House
81 Fulham Rd
London SW3

Design Museum
Butlers Wharf
Shad Thames
London SE1

Ikon Corporation
B5L Metropolitan Wharf
Wapping Wall
London E1

Maison Designs
917-919 Fulham Rd
London SW6

USA

Riccardo Rosa
1 West, 64 Street #8B
New York

Stending International
305 East 63rd Street
New York

guide to sources: books, catalogues, articles

ADIFAD *25 Años de Diseño Industrial: Los Premios Delta* (Barcelona, Gustav Gili, 1986)

Aguirre, Pere Interview with P.A. in *Informaciones* No. 18, Sept.–Oct. 1984, pp. 22–4 (Barcelona)

Anderson, Charles W. *The Political Economy of Modern Spain: Policy-Making in an Authoritarian System* (Wisconsin UP, 1970)

Ardi No. 4, July–Aug. 1988 (Barcelona). Monograph on Oscar Tusquets

Arnolfini Gallery (exh. cat.) *Photography and Posters of the Spanish Civil War* (Bristol, Arnolfini, 1986)

Arts Council (exh. cat.) *Homage to Barcelona: The city and its art, 1888–1936* (London, Arts Council, 1986)

Blanc, Antoni 'La Participación de FAD en Hogarotel' in *Hogares Modernos* No. 65, Jan. 1972, pp. 53–5 (Barcelona)

Bohigas, Oriol 'Altre Cop els Premis Delta' in *Serra d'Or* Year X, No. 100, Jan. 1968, pp. 65–6 (Montserrat)

Bohigas, Oriol *Contra una arquitectura adjetivada* (Barcelona, Seix Barral, 1969)

Bohigas, Oriol 'Bares, Discos, y Otras Amenidades por el Estilo' in *Arquitecturas Bis*, Dec. 1985 (Barcelona)

Bohigas, Oriol *Combat d'Incerteses: Dietari de Records* (Barcelona, Edicions 62, 1989)

Bonet Correa, Antonio (ed.) *Arte del Franquismo* (Madrid, Cuadernos Arte Cátedra, 1981)

Buchanan, Peter 'Spain: Poetics of Modernism' in *Architectural Review* Vol. CLXXIX, No. 1071, May 1986. Monograph on contemporary Spanish architecture

Campi i Valls, Isabel *Història del Disseny Industrial* (Barcelona, Col.leció Massana, Edicions 62, 1987). Final chapter devoted to industrial design in Catalonia

Carr, Raymond and Fusi, Juan Pablo *Spain: Dictatorship to Democracy* (London, Allen and Unwin, 1979)

Cirici, Alexandre 'L'art de la saviesa' in *Ariel*, Year 1, 1946, pp. 30–2 (Montpellier)

Cirici, Alexandre 'Dialegs d'Eina, El Grup 63 i l'avantguardia' in *Serra d'Or* Year IX, No. 3, March 1967, pp. 67–9 (227–9) (Montserrat)

Cirici, Alexandre 'La generaciò dels seixantes' in *Serra d'Or* Year XI, No. 121, Oct. 1969, pp. 67–9 (Montserrat)

Cirici, Alexandre *La Estética del Franquismo* (Barcelona, Gustavo Gili, 1977)

Clotet, Lluís 'Els Estudiants d'Arquitectura' in *Serra d'Or* Year IX, No. 7, July 1967, p. 33 (Montserrat)

Combalia, V., Suárez, A., and Vidal, M. 'Arte y transición politica el reflejo de un desfase' in *El Viejo Topo* (Barcelona) No. 11, Aug. 1977, pp. 60–3

Corredor Matheos, José 'El Diseño en España' in *CAU* Nos. 2–3, Sept. 1970, pp. 84–8 (Barcelona)

Design No. 469, Jan. 1988 (London). Monograph devoted to Spanish design

Domènech, Lluís 'Deltes del 1966' in *Serra d'Or* Year IX, No. 2, Feb. 1967, pp. 71–2 (Montserrat)

Domènech, Lluís *Arquitectura de Siempre* (Barcelona, Tusquets Editor, 1978)

Durán-Lóriga, Miguel 'ICSID, 1971, Ibiza' in *YA*, 28 Nov. 1971, reproduced in *Temas de Diseño* No. 1, March/April 1972, press section, p. 3 (Madrid)

Eina *Eina, escola de disseny i art, 1967–1987: Vint anys d'avantguardia* (Barcelona, Eina, 1987)

Formica (exh. cat.) *8 Diseñadores en ColorCore* (Vitoria, 1985)

Fundación BCD *Diseño Barcelona* (Barcelona, Fundación BCD, 1987)

Fundación BCD (exh. cat.) *Design in Catalogna* (Barcelona, Fundación BCD, 1988)

Fundación Foessa *Informe Sociologica Sobre la*

Situación Social de España (Madrid, Euramérica, 1975)

Garfias, Francisco 'Informe de la OCDE sobre la politica científica en España' in *Arbor* Vol. LXXXI, No. 313, Jan. 1972, pp. 97–101 (Madrid)

Generalitat de Catalunya *Llibre Blanc del Disseny a Catalunya Vol. 1 Disseny Industrial, Vol. 2. Disseny Grafic, Vol. 3 Disseny Artesà* (Barcelona, Generalitat de Catalunya, Dept. de la Presidencia Servei Central de Publicacions, 1984)

Generalitat de Catalunya *Barcelona, Paris, New York: El Camí de Dotze Artistes Catalans 1960–1980* (Generalitat de Catalunya, Dept. de Cultura, 1985)

Hooper, John *The Spaniards: A Portrait of the New Spain* (Harmondsworth, Penguin, 1986)

Julier, Guy Book reviews in *Journal of Design History* Vol. 2, No. 4, 1989, pp. 307–10

Julier, Guy 'Radical Modernism in Contemporary Spanish Design' in *Modernism in Design* (ed. Paul Greenhalgh) (London, Reaktion Books, 1990)

Liebermann, Sima *The Contemporary Spanish Economy: A Historical Perspective* (London, Allen and Unwin, 1982)

Lores, Jaume 'Diseño sin Industria' in *CAU* No. 11, Jan.–Feb. 1972, pp. 40–1 (Barcelona)

Mainar, Josep and Corredor-Matheos, Josep

Dels Bells Oficis – FAD 80 Anys – Al Disseny Actual (Barcelona, Editorial Blume, 1984)

Mañà, Jordi *El Diseño y la Exportación* (Barcelona, Centro de Estudios Internacional: Camara Oficial de Comercio, Industria y Navegacion de Barcelona, 2nd ed., 1983)

Mann, Claudia M.A. *Clotet/Tusquets* (Gustavo Gili, Barcelona, 1983)

Ministerio de Industria y Energia (exh. cat.) *Diseño Diseño* (Madrid, 1982)

Ministerio de Industria y Energia *España en Europa: Un Futuro Industrial* (Madrid, Ministerio de Industria y Energia, 1987)

Mir Pozo, Asunción *Evolución del Diseño Industrial y Datos Para su Estudio en Cataluña* (unpublished thesis for Licenciatura en Arte, Barcelona, 1974)

Rabat, Esperança 'El disseny i la industria catalana' in *El Mòn* 14–20 Jan. 1988, No. 299, pp. 38–41 (Barcelona)

Ricard, Andre *Hablando de diseño* (Barcelona, Punt de Vista, 1987)

Rivas, Manuel 'La tercera España' in *El Globo*, Madrid, No. 1, 9–15 Oct. 1987, pp. 30–41

Sabel, Charles F. *Work and Politics: The division of labor in industry* (Cambridge, Cambridge University Press, 1982)

San Martin, Eduardo 'La Conquista de la Modernidad' in *El Globo*, Madrid, No. 1, 9–15 Oct. 1987, p.7

Satué, Enric *El Disseny Gràfic a Catalunya* (Barcelona, Els llibres de la frontera, 1987)

Satué, Enric *El diseño gráfico: Desde los orígenes hasta nuestros días* (Madrid, Alianza Forma, 1988). Final chapter devoted to Spain

Sempere, Pedro and Corazón, Alberto *La Década Prodigiosa* (Madrid, Felmar, 1976)

Shaw, Duncan *Fútbol y Franquismo* (Prologo de Paul Preston) (Madrid, Alianza Editorial, 1987)

Suarez, Alicia and Vidal, Mercè 'De la "década prodigiosa" a "el sueño ha terminado"' in *El Descrédito de las Vanguardias Artisticas* by Combalia, V. and others, pp. 90–114 (Barcelona, Blume, 1980)

Suarez, Alicia and Vidal, Mercè 'Alexandre Cirici, Professor' in *Serra d'Or* Year XXV, No. 285, April 1983, pp. 30–1 (Montserrat)

Vázquez Montalbán, Manuel 'La Belle et La Bête ou les Années Trompeuses' in *Barcelone Baroque et Moderne: L'Exuberance Catalane*, pp. 22–30 (Paris, Editions Autrement, 1986)

Vila-San-Juan, Sergio 'El boom barcelonés visto por Alfredo Arribas: arquitectura y "disseny" para neófitos' in *Ajoblanco* No. 13, Jan. 1989, pp. 44–59 (Barcelona)

Wright, Alison *The Spanish Economy 1959–1975* (London, 1977)

acknowledgments

(i) Author

Firstly, thanks are due to Christopher Frayling and Penny Sparke at the Royal College of Art, London, for their initial encouragement in researching Spanish design, which later led to this book. Also to Helen Rees and staff at the Design Museum, London. Particular thanks should go to numerous friends in Spain: Montserrat Castro and Mariona Solé; Juan Ramón Ferrandis; and especially the Cases family – Francesc, Tere, Laeia and Mireia; Isabel Campi for her help with the more obscure parts of the picture research; and Anna Maio and Mª Angels Pujol at the International Design Press Agency in Barcelona.

Much of this book was developed through formal interviews and informal conversations with many people, among them the following, whose patience and enthusiasm I warmly acknowledge: Fernando Amat (Vinçon); José Mª Aznar, Angel Martí, José Fco, Sánchez and Carlos Tíscar (Factoria Diseño Industrial); Paco Bascuñán, Sandra Figuerola and Marisa Gallén (La Nave); Txema García Amiano (Akaba); Bigas Luna; Joan Antoni Blanc; Guillermo Capdevila; Juli Capella and Quim Larrea (*Ardi*); Frederico Correa; Josep Mª Civit; Pepe Cortés; Jane Dillon; Mai Felip (BCD); Mª Carmen Ferrer (Via Design); J. García Garay (García Garay); Mercè Bohigas and Marti Gascon (Miscel.lània de Mercè Bohigas); Pepe Gimeno; Ramón Isern; Alberto Liévore; Josep Lluscà; Jordi Mañà; Vicent Martínez (Punt Mobles); Miguel Milà; Arcadi Moradell (A.M.A.); Javier Nieto and Gabriel Ordeig (Santa & Cole); Pati Nuñez; Jorge Pensi; Peret; André Ricard; Carlos Riart; Carlos Riera (Disform); Román Riera (Metalarte); Nancy Robbins; Eduardo Samsó; América Sánchez; Pep Sant (Asssociate Designers); Enric Satué; Amparo Sena (IMPIVA); Josep Mª Tremoleda (Mobles 114); Jaime Tresserra; Josep Mª Trias (Quod).

Finally, thanks to Thames and Hudson, and, of course, Sue Santilhano and our son, Joseph, for patience and understanding.

(ii) Illustrations

Alfredo Arribas: 120, 134, 154–5 (all), 156–7 (all) (photos Jordi Sarrà), 158 (photos Jordi Sarrà and Hisao Suzuki); Archivo ADIFAD, Barcelona: 161, 164; *Arquitectura*, Madrid: 24; Associate Designers, Barcelona: 172–3 (all); Barcelona Centre de Disseny: 35; Josep Bagà: 106 (all); Isabel Campi: 23, 31, 33, 45, 126, 137 (top right); Lluís Casals: 137 (bottom left and right), 141, 144–5, 146–7; Ron Charlesworth: 123, 129; Contrapunto, Madrid: 119; Disform, Barcelona: 67 (all); Factoria Diseño Industrial, Valencia: 168; Ferran Freixa: 138–9 (all), 140, 148 (left and top), 149; García Garay, Barcelona: 85 (all); Pepe Gimeno: 118; *Hogares Modernos*, Barcelona: 131; Institut Municipal d'Història, Barcelona: 25, 27, 29; International Design Press Agency, Barcelona: 9 (top), 12, 14–15, 16, 24, 39, 48, 49, 54, 59, 61, 68, 69, 74 (left), 75, 76–7 (all), 82–3 (all), 84, 86–7 (all), 160, 165, 169, 170, 171 (bottom); Albert Isern: 107 (right); Guy Julier: 19, 22, 42 (left), 50, 58, 124, 125, 137 (top left); Liberty's, London: 72–3, 74 (top right), 78–9, 176; Pedro Mandueño: 143 (bottom left); Mariscal: 112–13 (all), 142–3 (right, photo Jordi Sarrà); Miscel.lània de Mercè Bohigas, Barcelona: 168 (all); Arcadi Moradell: 103; Museu d'Història de la Ciutat, Barcelona: 122; La Nave, Madrid: 9 (bottom), 13, 114 (all), 115 (all), 174 (all); Peret: 89, 108 (all), 109 (all); Punt Mobles, Valencia: 80–1 (all); Quod Diseño y Marketing, Barcelona: 97, 111, 171 (top); Carlos Rolando: 116–17 (all); Eduardo Samsó: 6, 10, 133, 152–3 (photos Jordi Sarrà); América Sánchez: 95; Santa & Cole, Barcelona: 51, 65 (top), 70–1 (all), 148, 150–1 (all); Jordi Sarrà: 65 (left); Enric Satué: 11, 90, 91, 92, 104, 162; SEAT, Britain: 163; Studio Per, Barcelona: 32; Patrocinio Soriano: 159; Taula de Disseny, Barcelona: 101; Jaime Tresserra: 40, 66; Via Design, Barcelona: 175 (all); Vinçon, Barcelona: 42, 43 (right, photo Loles Duran).

index